T0274564

Romeo and Juliet

The Applause Shakespeare Workbook Series

OTHER SHAKESPEARE TITLES FROM APPLAUSE

Once More unto the Speech Dear Friends
in three volumes: *The Comedies, The Histories, The Tragedies*
Compiled and Edited with Commentary by Neil Freeman

Monologues from Shakespeare's First Folio
in twelve volumes: *The Comedies, The Histories, The Tragedies for Any Gender,*
Older Men, Women, and Younger Men
Compiled with Commentary by Neil Freeman, Edited by Paul Sugarman

The Applause First Folio in Modern Type
Prepared and Annotated by Neil Freeman

The Folio Texts
Prepared and Annotated by Neil Freeman
Each of the 36 plays of the Applause First Folio in Modern Type, individually bound

The Applause Shakespeare Library
Plays of Shakespeare Edited for Performance
John Russell Brown, series editior

Shakescenes: Shakespeare for Two by John Russell Brown

Free Shakespeare by John Russell Brown

Shakespeare's Plays in Performance by John Russell Brown

Shakespeare: A Popular Life by Garry O'Connor

The Actor and the Text by Cicely Berry

Acting Shakespeare by John Gielgud

Soliloquy: The Shakespeare Monologues
Co-edited by Michael Earley and Philippa Keil

Romeo and Juliet

The Applause Shakespeare Workbook Series

Commentary by
John Russell Brown and Neil Freeman

Edited by Paul Sugarman

APPLAUSE
THEATRE & CINEMA BOOKS
Essex, Connecticut

APPLAUSE
THEATRE & CINEMA BOOKS

An imprint of Globe Pequot, the trade division of
The Rowman & Littlefield Publishing Group, Inc.
4501 Forbes Blvd., Ste. 200
Lanham, MD 20706
www.rowman.com

Distributed by NATIONAL BOOK NETWORK

Copyright © 2023 by Applause Theatre & Cinema Books

Material drawn from *Shakescenes: Shakespeare for Two*
Copyright © 1992 Applause Theatre Book Publishers

Material drawn from *Once More Unto the Speech Dear Friends*
Copyright © 2006 Folio Scripts, Vancouver Canada

Material drawn from *Romeo and Juliet: The Applause Shakespeare Library*
Copyright © 2002 Applause Books

Introduction and other additional material © 2023 Paul Sugarman

All rights reserved. No part of this book may be reproduced in any form or by any electronic or mechanical means, including information storage and retrieval systems, without written permission from the publisher, except by a reviewer who may quote passages in a review.

Library of Congress Cataloging-in-Publication Data

Names: Brown, John Russell, author. | Freeman, Neil, author. | Sugarman, Paul, editor.
Title: Romeo and Juliet / commentary by John Russell Brown and Neil Freeman ; edited by Paul Sugarman.
Description: Lanham, MD : Applause Theatre & Cinema Books, 2023. | Series: The Applause Shakespeare Workbook Series
Identifiers: LCCN 2023029585 (print) | LCCN 2023029586 (ebook) | ISBN 9781493057009 (pbk.) | ISBN 9781493057016 (ebk.)
Subjects: LCSH: Shakespeare, William, 1564–1616. Romeo and Julet. | Shakespeare, William, 1564–1616—Dramatic production.
Classification: LCC PR2831 .B76 2023 (print) | LCC PR2831 (ebook) | DDC 822.3/3—dc23/eng/20230706
LC record available at https://lccn.loc.gov/2023029585
LC ebook record available at https://lccn.loc.gov/2023029586

♾️™ The paper used in this publication meets the minimum requirements of American National Standard for Information Sciences—Permanence of Paper for Printed Library Materials, ANSI/NISO Z39.48-1992.

CONTENTS

OVERVIEW: WORKING ON SHAKESPEARE TO BUILD TOWARD PERFORMANCE

Perform the Text: Share the text with a wider audience.

Share the Text: Speak the text to someone else.

Action: Find the Choices in the Text: What choices can be made in terms of the character?

Explore the Text: Consult the First Folio to see how capitalization, punctuation, and line endings can shift emphasis. Connect to the text physically and personally.

Analyze the Text: Look at the text in depth to see how it works. Is it verse or prose?

Understand the Text: You need to understand what is being said and what all the words mean.

Read the Text Aloud: These words were meant to be spoken.

INTRODUCTION

Paul Sugarman

The aim of this Applause Shakespeare Workbook is to provide tools for working on the text of *Romeo and Juliet*. Out of the many Applause publications on Shakespeare this book draws material from the works of John Russell Brown (*Shakescenes* and the Applause Shakespeare Library) and Neil Freeman (*Once More Unto the Speech* series and the Folio Texts) to give you and/or your actors or students practical approaches to work on the text.

These plays, while they speak much to our human condition today, are from more than four hundred years ago. To fully appreciate Shakespeare, there is a lot that one needs to know. There are many books published by Applause that can help you understand and work on Shakespeare. First you need to understand the time when he lived, which has similarities to today and many differences. *William Shakespeare: A Popular Life* by Garry O'Connor gives insight into Shakespeare's time. Much like Stephen Greenblatt's *Will in the World*, it paints a picture of Shakespeare's age and makes connections between that time and the text in his plays that give a broader perspective on the images and references in Shakespeare's works.

There is the need for much more in-depth study and work on how to use your voice to speak the text. Applause publishes *The Actor and the Text* by Cicely Berry, which reveals how Shakespeare uses language to express so much in such a wide variety of ways and the need to have a strong and connected voice to be able to do it justice. She includes hands-on approaches to the text to show how Shakespeare uses rhetoric to make his points. Her *Working Shakespeare* video series shows many top UK and US actors putting her techniques into practice.

There is also the practicality of how to understand his work in performance. One of John Russell Brown's central ideas is that you can't fully understand and appreciate Shakespeare without understanding how it works in performance. He wrote many books on Shakespeare and many editions of the works of Shakespeare and other early modern playwrights. Applause has published many of his books including

Shakescenes, which provides material for this book; and *Shakespeare's Plays in Performance*, which looks at performance elements and performance history. *Free Shakespeare* contrasts how the plays were originally performed with the vision of the actor-based ensembles, which has been influential for many American acting companies. John Russell Brown created the Applause Shakespeare Library, which included theatrical commentary to make sure that performance considerations are an essential part of studying the play. There is also much that can be gained from great performers of Shakespeare as shown by John Gielgud's books *Acting Shakespeare* and *An Actor and His Time*, as well as the many fine biographies of great stage actors such as Gielgud, Laurence Olivier, and Ralph Richardson, also published by Applause.

The importance of the first collected publication of Shakespeare's plays, the First Folio of 1623, cannot be underestimated. It collected thirty-six of Shakespeare's plays, eighteen of which had never been published before and would have been lost forever. Applause published all thirty-six plays from the First Folio in individual editions that were prepared and annotated by Neil Freeman. Applause published the single volume *The Applause First Folio of Shakespeare in Modern Type*. Freeman then went on to create the *Once More Unto the Speech* series of books comparing modern and Folio texts for more than nine hundred speeches, demonstrating the practicality of using Folio texts. Material from that series has been made more accessible in the recent series of *Monologues from Shakespeare's First Folio* series of twelve books. Neil Freeman was one of the major forces in making the First Folio more useful for actors and students of the plays.

Both John Russell Brown and Neil Freeman were champions for understanding Shakespeare through performance. John Russell Brown's Applause Shakespeare Library was designed to make one aware of the many opportunities presented by the text for performance. Neil Freeman's First Folio texts showed the many clues and choices that could be explored through looking at the text as originally printed. By taking examples from both men's work, these materials present different perspectives on the text.

The wonderful thing about working on Shakespeare is that there is no one "right" answer. His work endures because it is so flexible and subject to varied interpretations. In your own exploration of the text you have to find which choices work best for you (and, perhaps, your students). To find the best choice you need to explore what is out there and why these more than four-hundred-year-old texts still speak to us today.

This workbook presents a brief description of various approaches to the text by John Russell Brown and Neil Freeman. Following are scenes from the play that John Russell Brown had included in *Shakescenes* along with further selections from the Applause Shakespeare Library edition of the play. Speeches from the play drawn from Neil Freeman's *Once More Unto the Speech* series will give a First Folio perspective on the text.

The goal is to be able to speak and share Shakespeare's words in a way that makes the plays come alive in ways they do not when read silently. Perhaps the biggest perceived challenge is understanding and getting comfortable with Shakespeare's language. Though the language may seem old to us, the English language of Shakespeare was four hundred years *younger* then than it is now, as Kristin Linklater, author of *Freeing Shakespeare's Voice*, observed. Although these words are from four centuries ago, it is still Modern English but in its infancy, when it was still blossoming and expanding. The spoken word was essential to almost all communication in Shakespeare's day, unlike our predominantly visual and text-based age. We don't talk as much or as precisely as those whose lives depended on spoken communication in Shakespeare's time. Shakespeare does a lot more with language than we do in our modern world. Working on Shakespeare's language can open one up to new and more effective ways of communicating. These great thoughts and words show the possibilities of expression that a human voice can achieve.

Basic Steps to Working on Shakespeare's Text

Read the Text Aloud: These words were meant to be spoken. Music cannot be experienced solely by looking at annotations on a page. Neither can Shakespeare.

Understand the Text: You need to understand what is being said and what all the words mean. It is important to consult glossaries that give Elizabethan definitions and context. David and Ben Crystal's website shakespeareswords.com is a good place to start.

Analyze the Text: Look at the text in depth to see how it works. Is it verse or prose? If verse, where is it regular and where not? Shakespeare uses rhetorical devices to convey feelings and meanings. How do the sounds and words "play" off each other?

Explore the Text: Consult the First Folio to see how capitalization, punctuation, and line endings can shift emphasis. Connect to the text physically and personally. How do the words and sounds feel inside your body?

Action: Find the Choices in the Text: What choices can be made in terms of the character? What actions can they take? What choices can be made about their needs? Some choices may seem obvious, but look for the possibilities of different ones.

Share the Text: Speak the text to someone else so that you can assess how well you are communicating the thoughts beneath the text.

Perform the Text: Share the text with a wider audience, to whom you can also speak directly, as there was no fourth wall in Shakespeare's theater.

Committing to speaking Shakespeare's text requires more of us than most contemporary communication does. Energize the whole body when giving voice to the text. There have been many fine books on using the voice to support Shakespeare text work including *The Actor and the Text* by Cicely Berry (Applause) and *Freeing Shakespeare's Voice* by Kristin Linklater (TCG).

The exploration of the text can continue indefinitely as there is no one answer to these texts but an endless array of possibilities to be explored. However, if you start with speaking and listening instead of just reading the words, it will lead you to a more personal connection to the text.

Shakespeare connects to so many people in different ways because we find something in our personal lives that is explained by the way Shakespeare says it. Sometimes the text instantly makes sense to you, but often the possibilities are infinite. We make choices based on how the text connects to us at this moment in our time.

This workbook will outline some of the tools to look at the text and give examples from the works of John Russell Brown and Neil Freeman, who can offer differing viewpoints on the same text as a way for you to learn to trust your ear and your connection to the text. This workbook will show ways to work on the text with a spirit of exploration.

ADVICE TO ACTORS

John Russell Brown

There is no such person as a "Shakespearean actor," if that phrase implies the possession of unique qualifications or unusual gifts. Shakespeare's plays are available to all good actors, no matter what their training or experience may be.

Yet, of course, the texts reprinted here are not like those of modern plays. Shakespeare does present special problems, and the blunt assurance that his writing is open for anyone to explore will not sound very convincing to a student-actor meeting it for the first time. The following approaches are offered as encouragement to make a start and free imagination to work intelligently on the texts.

Character

First of all, an actor in any play must discover the person behind the words of any particular role. Of course, an actor must learn how to speak the character's lines clearly and forcefully, but that alone will not bring the play to life. Speech is not all, because Shakespeare did not write for talking heads. He first imagined individual persons in lively interplay with each other and *then* conjured words for them to speak; and that is the best sequence for an actor to follow. A living person has to be brought to the stage, and then he can begin to speak and become realized in the process.

In Elizabethan times, plays were performed on a large platform stage that jutted out into the middle of a crowded audience, many of whom were standing rather than sitting as is the custom today; and in this open arena everything took place by daylight. Some performances were given indoors, but then the audience was illuminated along with the actors. Such conditions were more like those of a public meeting in our day, or of a booth in a fairground. They called for an acting style that was grounded in a basic physical delineation of each character. An actor had to maintain the vibrant outlines of the role so that his performance could be viewed from all sides and at all times whenever he was on stage.

11

Character Questions

BASIC QUESTIONS:

- How does the character move and speak?

- How think and feel?

- Where does this individual come from? What does he know? What does he want?

- What does he look like, sound like?

- How could anyone recognize the person who speaks these lines?

- Why does this particular person need to speak these particular words?

- How old is this person?

- What physical characteristics are essential for an impersonation?

- What is this person's family situation?

- What are the political, professional, and social conditions of his life?

MORE DIFFICULT QUESTIONS FOLLOW, WHICH HELP TO DEFINE PERSONALITY AND CONSCIOUSNESS:

- How does this person "see" and respond to the world around him?

- What does he like and dislike? What does he pursue and what does he seek to avoid?

- What conventions, social pressures, or political forces influence behavior, either consciously or unconsciously?

INTERROGATING THE TEXT:

- What verbs does the character use?

- How does he talk to other characters?

- Do questions, assertions, explanations, answers, excuses, qualifications, elaborations, or repetitions predominate?

- Are sentences long or short, leisured and assured, or compact and urgent?

- Are sentences governed by a single main verb?

- Or are they supplied with a sequence of phrases, each governed by its own subsidiary verb?

- How does this person refer to others: always in the same way, or with variations? With different names, titles, or endearments?

- Is address intimate or formal, simple or elaborate?

- Or is contact between two characters assumed and assured, so that names are not required at all?

Normally such detailed verbal enquiry is a continuous process that goes on throughout a long rehearsal period. Scrutiny of every word in even a short scene will help to develop a sensitivity to words, a facility that can be drawn upon constantly throughout an actor's career in whatever plays he may perform.

ALL KINDS OF EXERCISES CAN HELP:

- Very slow rehearsals encourage full awareness of what is thought and felt, as the words are spoken easily without thought of projecting or shaping them.

- Silent rehearsals, with someone else speaking the text.

- Improvised explorations of moments of encounter or retreat.

- Improvised paraphrasing of Shakespeare's text.

- Sessions in which the actors sit back-to-back and only speak the words, trying to communicate fully.

- Variations in positions, so that the two actors are at first close and then far apart, quite still and then always on the move, looking at each other or refusing to do so, paying attention to nothing but the sound of words or engaged on other business—all these explorations may find new means of expression or more physical enactments for a scene.

- Questions should be asked, as for any play, to encourage a fuller sense of what is afoot in a scene: What do they expect from each other? How secure or insecure are they?

What we can deduce about Elizabethan stage practice should encourage present-day actors to seek out distinctive physical characteristics for each role they play in Shakespeare, possess or embody them as fully as possible, and then play the text boldly. This will provide the appropriate dynamic and credibility.

The moment actors walk onto the stage in character, they must be strong and expressive, even before a word has been spoken. Then as each person is drawn into the drama, there must be no loss of definition but growth, development, and surprise. As the play continues, new facets and new resources will be revealed, until each character has become fully present and open to an audience. In performance, actors need to be alert and active and must possess great reserves of energy. They are like boxers in a ring who dare not lose concentration or the ability to perform at full power. They have to watch, listen, move, and speak, and at the same time embody the persons they represent. It is like levitating, or flying through the air, by a continuous act of will and imagination. Characters must have clarity; actors, courage.

But how can an actor find the person to present? Trial and error play no small role in shaping a trained instinct for Shakespeare's people. And this trial begins with a close interrogation of the text.

In a search for the person to bring onstage, first impressions may be deceptive or, rather, limiting. For example, on a first reading, Romeo and Juliet may appear to be two "typical" romantic lovers who delight in each other's presence and have much in common, including parents who would disapprove very strongly of their love if they were to know of it. All that is true and useful, but if the two actors for these roles were each to make a list of the nouns in their respective speeches, two very different sensibilities and personalities would be revealed. The minds of Romeo and Juliet run in different directions; they have their own sensations and feelings, and distinct views of the world around them.

There are many constructive ways of studying Shakespeare's words beyond tracing verb patterns. Preparing lists of adjectives and adverbs may reveal when and where a character is sufficiently thoughtful to qualify an idea, although some speakers in some scenes will never have sufficient command or perception to use a qualifying or descriptive word. Lists of double meanings, similes, metaphors, references to other realities than the one on-stage—whether the imagined world is distant, intimate, literary, political, religious, or historical—can help to show the deeper resources of a character's mind.

Slowly, by such analysis of the text, a psychological "identikit" can be assembled, marking predominant colors, preconceptions, modes of thought and feeling. Many such separate and small details begin to suggest a more embracing idea about a person.

On the other hand, it would be a mistake to read and analyze for too long; an actor needs to start to act and to speak just as soon as intuition and imagination are quickened by more deliberate investigations. The actor's own being has to be satisfied and used in performance, as well as the details of the text.

Slowly, a sense of the character's consciousness will emerge, and a number of physical traits will become established. So, the stage character should evolve slowly, from within itself, freshly and uniquely created; actions will suit the words and reveal a sense of being that attracts and repays attention. There is no knowing what may happen. One danger is that too many details will attract attention so that the basic presence is left undeveloped. After making his discoveries, the actor must therefore decide which of his discoveries are truly necessary and which can be discarded.

Careful and patient study, analysis, exploration, imitation, quiet impulse, quick imagination, and the luck of adventurous rehearsal all have a contribution to make in the creation of these plays.

Verse, Prose, and Language

Laurence Olivier in his portrayal of the lead in *Henry the Fifth* decided to be real, rather than phony, grand, or rhetorical. So he "got underneath the lines," and in rehearsal his acting became so close to natural behavior that the words were sometimes indistinct and difficult to hear. Then one day, Tyrone Guthrie, the director, stopped the rehearsal—he had been away for a while and insisted that this actor should perform the verse and the rhetoric: "Larry . . . let's have it properly," he called out from the back of the theater. For a moment, Olivier hesitated and then did as he was told; and the change, as he tells the story, was instantaneous and transforming. He had always known that verse and sentence structure, and imagery, were instructing him to speak with confidence, enjoyment, and resonance, and that they had a commanding and developing power, but he had held back in distrust. Now he found that artificial verse and grand language fitted his character like necessary and proper clothes, and they gave him the ability to rouse his audience on stage and in the auditorium. (When he came to act the part in the film, they even roused his horse.) Olivier was still truth-ful, but now he was also heroic.

Poetry is the natural idiom of Shakespeare's stage, as swimming is for the ocean, singing for opera or musical theater, controlled and exceptional movement for dance, or solemnity for great occasions. Speaking Shake-speare's verse becomes as instinctive as song, and the actor forgets that he is being metrically correct and vocally subtle.

Elizabethan audiences were so convinced by performances in which verse was spoken that a play written wholly in prose would be more likely to seem artificial. Today Shakespeare's plays can become *just* as real, if actors both use the verse and also act with truth to life. Bernard Shaw advised actors in Shakespeare's early plays to treat the verse like a child does a swing, without self-consciousness or hesitation. In later plays the art of verse is more demanding and the pleasure it gives deeper, but both must be similarly instinctive.

Until verse speaking has become second nature—as it quite quickly does—an actor should study the meter of the lines well in advance of rehearsals, methodically picking out the words to be stressed and find-ing, by trial and error, the most appropriate phrasing. It is necessary to speak the lines out loud, so that meaning and syntax can be related to the demands of versification and *vice versa*. Breathing and speaking should work together so that the energy of thought and feeling responds to the text and begins to motivate speech. Texture, linked variations of sound, alliteration, assonance, rhyme, and rhythm must all be heeded. These concepts cannot be explored fully in the mind. By speaking the words, their sounds and visceral impact will reveal different levels of meaning. Phrasing, breathing, tempo, pace, pitch, intonation, silence have all to be considered. The lines must be spoken aloud again and again, as one way of speaking is tested against another; and then, slowly, by following the clues inherent in the text, a fully responsive delivery can emerge.

When using this book, start to "do" whenever doubt arises. Genera-tions of actors will assure you that with practice, the acting of Shake-speare's poetry—not merely the speaking of it—becomes instinctive and fluent, pleasurable and, in the context of the play, both true and natural.

The actor should begin by appreciating Shakespeare's preferred medium, the iambic pentameter. Each line should have ten syllables, alter-nately weak and strong, so that each pair of syllables forms one "foot," and five feet complete a line. Although few pentameters are entirely regular—

if they were, the dialogue would be unbearably wooden and predictable—all follow the ongoing pattern to some degree. It is their likeness that links them together, while their irregularity draws attention to particular words, varies rhythm and pace, and lends a forward movement to speech as disturbance of pattern awakens an expectation that pattern will be reasserted and finally satisfied.

STEPS TO ANALYZING THE TEXT

- Is it verse or prose?
- If verse, is it regular or irregular? Many lines are irregular with stresses not following the iambic pattern or if there are other than ten syllables in a line.
- Speak the text to find the most natural emphasis.

Sense, syntax, speakability, and an underlying regularity are the principal guides in scanning a line, but they do not always provide an unequivocal lead. Until well-practiced in verse speaking, a student should mark the text in pencil, changing the stresses until sure enough to start rehearsals. Still more changes may be made later, before this slow and methodical preparation can be forgotten and taken for granted—that is the last and absolutely necessary part of the process.

Scansion

In deciding how to scan a line, some general rules may be applied. Nouns and verbs always need to be stressed in order to make the sense clear—more stressed than adjectives, adverbs, pronouns, prepositions, or conjunctions. Moreover the fourth syllable of any line, being the most able to reestablish the normal pattern after irregularities and most in control of each individual line, is nearly always stressed in a regular way. If the end of a line is irregular, the beginning of the following one is likely to be regular, for two, or three, consecutive feet. However, the first foot in a line is very frequently irregular, since a reversed foot, with the strong syllable coming first, gives fresh impetus to new thought.

An example from an early play gives clear indication of both regularity and irregularity:

(King Edward speaks to his queen about political enemies.)

  ˘   —   ˘ — ˘ — ˘ ˘ —   —
My love, forbear to fawn upon their frowns.

    ˘   — ˘ —   ˘ ˘ — ˘ — ˘   ˘
What danger or what sorrow can befall thee

  ˘   — ˘ — ˘ — ˘   — ˘   —
So long as Edward is thy constant friend

    ˘   —   ˘   —   ˘   —   ˘   —   ˘ —
And their true sovereign whom they must obey?

    —   ˘   ˘   — ˘ — ˘   —   —   —
Nay, whom they shall obey, and love thee too,   5

  ˘   —   ˘   —   ˘   — ˘ ˘ —   —
Unless they seek for hatred at my hands-

    ˘   — ˘ —   ˘ ˘ —   ˘ —
Which if they do, yet will I keep thee safe

  ˘   —   ˘ — ˘ — ˘ ˘ —
And they shall feel the vengeance of my wrath.

(Henry VI, Part lll, IV.i.75–82)

Some of the strong stresses marked in these lines might be changed, but
very few; and all its irregularities are brief. The close of line 5 is most prob-
lematical: it is marked here with three consecutive strong syllables as the
sense of the parenthesis seems to require, but the final "too" might be
unstressed or, possibly, the penultimate "thee." (Three consecutive strong
stresses should be used very sparingly, because they doubly disturb the
underlying norm.) A similar uncertainty arises at the end of line 2, which
is marked here with the final "thee" as an extra unstressed syllable. Alternatively, "can" would not be stressed and "befall" counted as a single strong
syllable, so that "thee" could follow with equal stress.

All the strong syllables are not equally stressed in speech, and here
actors have much more liberty to find the emphasis that suits their own
interpretation of a character. Many choices are available. In most iambic
pentameters only three syllables take major emphasis, the other stressed
syllables being only slightly more prominent than the unstressed ones. So
one reading of the same passage might be:

My love, *forbear* to *fawn* upon their *frowns.*
What *danger* or what sorrow can *befall* thee

So *long* as Edward is thy constant friend
And their true sovereign whom they *must obey?*
Nay, whom they *shall* obey, and *love thee* too,
Unless they *seek* for *hatred* at my *hands*
Which if they *do,* yet will I *keep* thee *safe*
And they shall feel the *vengeance* of my *wrath.*

Perhaps the first line should have four major emphases, as Edward presses his argument. In line 3, "constant" may be more significant than "long" and so take the emphasis; but the "f" in *friend* makes that word able to gain strength from the other stressed *f*s in the preceding lines. Choice of stress will also be influenced by words set either in opposition to contrast with each other or in agreement to reinforce each other. Stressing these words can often clarify the logic of what the speaker is saying. For example, in line 4, "their" might be stressed and the penultimate foot reversed, so that "they" is stressed as well for reinforcement, and "must" would count only as a weak syllable. Such a reading would raise the possibility that in line 7, "thee" might be stressed rather than "keep," so that the "they" in line 8 could be a fourth major emphasis in contrast with "thee," to bring a relatively sturdy finish to the whole speech. But, in general, pronouns should not be emphasized, because that takes away prominence from the nouns and verbs, which have to sustain the sense of any speech; those are the elements that form the supporting backbone for strong dialogue and provide its thought-action and forward impetus.

This simple speech of eight lines illustrates how metrical consider-ations become, very quickly and necessarily, issues of character as well. The same is true when problems of phrasing are introduced. In the early verse plays especially, a brief pause at the end of each line is usual and provides a further guide to phrasing beyond those inherent in sense and syntax. Yet this is not a constant rule, and sometimes only the slightest rise of pitch or marking of a final consonant is sufficient indication of a line-ending; in this way, two consecutive lines will run into each other almost without hesitation or change of impression. In this passage, if Edward pauses slightly after "friend," the last word of line 3, and after "safe" at the end of line 8, his thoughts of "love" will seem more urgent than those concerning political power because, in this reading, the latter will seem to be afterthoughts. But if line 3 runs over into line 4, with-out the customary pause at the line-ending, the two reactions become almost inseparable; and then the political motivation will outweigh the amorous, because it is expressed in a longer phrase and placed in a climactic position. The relationship between lines 7 and 8 raises similar possibilities.

A pause, or caesura, may also be marked in mid-line. Syntax or sense will sometimes require this to be done (as in line 7 above), but here too a choice is often to be made. The advantage of a mid-line break is that it can give a sense of ongoing thought and quick intelligence. Some critics would argue that every line should have its caesura, but there is good reason not to supply them too strongly or too consistently; such readings encourage a halting delivery and an impression of weakness, and are not always easy to comprehend. In this passage, the final line would clearly be stronger if there were no hint of a pause in mid-line. So might line 2—unless two slight pauses were given, as if commas had been placed after both "danger" and "sorrow," thus giving Edward a very thoughtful and determined manner of speech. Line 6 also seems to run without a break, unless it came after "seek," so giving point to Edward's personal involvement. Seldom should a mid-line pause be placed so that it breaks up a regular iambic foot; normally it should follow, and therefore still further emphasize, a strong syllable. If a caesura is marked in each line of this passage, a general impression of energetic thought might be given, and in some performances this could be useful.

No decision is solely a technical matter; versification in Shakespeare's mind was an instrument for enhancing a representation of individual characters in lively interplay. Problems of verse-speaking are truly dramatic problems, and so each actor must find solutions that suit his or her own impersonation. Although there are many ways of speaking verse that are clearly wrong—too many stressed syllables one after another is a common fault, and too few clear stresses another—there is no one correct way to speak any speech. A respect for versification offers many opportunities to strengthen one's grasp of the play in action and deepen the rendering of a character's very being.

As in any lifelike dialogue in prose, the actor must ask why speak at all; that is, he must discover and follow the action of thought and feeling beneath the words, sustaining and shaping them. In other terms, syntax is, in the last analysis, more important than meter. Each complete sentence is a distinct action, requiring breath, physical response, and speech, according to its own impulses.

In prose dialogue, sentence structure is the principal means whereby Shakespeare controls and so strengthens an actor's speaking of his text. Often the formal arrangement is very elaborate and sustained. Moreover, its effect is reinforced by the use of a series of parallel phrases and by wordplay; these both hold the subsections together and provide a sense of growth and climax. Exploring how the words play off each other in these ways can reveal the character's intentions. Stressing key words, puns, and affirmations is not enough; the flow and energy of the language have to be represented in performance, giving a sense of exploration, energy, struggle, attainment, frustration. Sentence structure and wordplay define this music and this drama, and the actor must respond to both and transmit both through performance.

Each actor must make his own distinctive response to the challenge of the text. No teacher or director can provide ready-made and sufficient solutions here, and this realization may help to understand something fundamental about the acting of Shakespeare: no instruction can take responsibility away from the actors. Sometimes students are recommended to speak Shakespeare's lines with a certain quality or tone of voice, or a certain accent, and for some exercises or some productions this may be useful. But following such a prescription is likely to do more harm than good, because the actor is distracted from the primary task of finding a voice and being for each character and then responding to the text in his or her own manner. Of course, efficient breathing and voice production are needed to respond to so demanding a text, but technical expertise must always be at the service of the specific demands of character, situation, and speech, as these are discovered by each individual actor.

Some words and phrases in the plays seem to cry out for a great deal of preparatory work, but it may be only a small exaggeration to say that every word, phrase, sentence, and speech may repay in some measure a similar investment. An actor can have an endless adventure when acting Shakespeare, as step by step he gets closer to a fully responsive, individual, and necessary (and therefore convincing) way of turning text into performance.

An actor's mind and body need to be more than usually alert and energized to answer the challenge. What starts as patient and complicated exploration can end, however, in a marvelous extension of an actor's powers of thought, feeling, and being, as the poetry comes to fresh and brilliant life. That is why Shakespeare's plays are so rewarding to perform. By making each word sound as if it is necessary to his or her character, an actor will claim attention with amazing ease.

Towards Performance

All kinds of exercises can help inexperienced actors. Very slow rehearsals encourage full awareness of what is thought and felt, as the words are spoken easily without thought of projecting or shaping them. Silent rehearsals, with someone else speaking the text, improvised explorations of moments of encounter or retreat, improvised paraphrasing of Shakespeare's text, or sessions in which the actors sit back-to-back and only speak the words, trying to communicate fully—all these devices may help performers to become more free, adventurous, and true. Variations in positions, so that the two actors are at first close and then far apart, quite still and then always on the move, looking at each other or refusing to do so, paying attention to nothing but the sound of words or engaged on other business—all these explorations may find new means of expression or more physical enactments for a scene. Questions should be asked, as for any play, to encourage a fuller sense of what is afoot in a scene: What do they expect from each other? How secure or insecure are they? Many of these questions were first asked in individual preparation. None of these ordinary ways of working is foreign to Shakespeare's plays.

When performing modern plays, actors have extensive stage directions in the text to guide them: descriptions of activity, unspoken reactions, movements, pauses, silences, and so on. But in Shakespeare's plays there is little of this, and what is printed in modern editions is often the invention of editors and not what Shakespeare wrote. In the versions of scenes printed in this book, stage directions are very scarce and minimal, but the commentary will often point out activity, movement and responses, that *may* be required for acting the text.

Actors must learn to read Shakespeare's stage directions implicit in the dialogue: clues for tempo, rhythm change, breathing, for closeness or distance between the characters, and so on. Very important, because usually unambiguous, is Shakespeare's use of incomplete verse lines to indicate a pause or silence in the middle of speech, or in the interchange between two people. When two characters share a single verse line, each speaking one half of a regular iambic pentameter, the opposite is true; there should be no pause or hesitation here, the dialogue continuing without break and the new speaker responsive to the phrasing, rhythm, and pitch of the person he follows.

So much can be discovered while working together on a text that simplification must become part of the ongoing process. Actors must identify those elements that are truest and most revealing and develop those at the cost of losing others. The essential part of this process is to recognize what is particularly alive and new in the work and take the necessary steps to allow this to grow.

There is a paradox at the heart of what can be said about the task of acting Shakespeare's plays. Imaginatively the performers need to be exceptionally free, and yet the most liberating work will be found by paying strict attention to the minutest details of the text and using them as spurs to invention and exploration. Shakespeare's imagination seems always to be ahead of ours, beckoning us; and so, if the actor is patient and adventurous, he will find within the text whatever suits his or her individual abilities and point of view. The text can be ever new, and even the most experienced actor or playgoer is liable to be amazed at what is achieved for the first time with any new production.

Of course, actors develop particular ways of working, and their interpretations of a number of roles will have much in common, but it is wise to beware of drawing the possibilities of a Shakespeare text down to the level of performance that a particular actor has found to be reliable. Shakespeare's kings are all different from each other, and so are his fools; and each one is liable to have a different life from scene to scene, sometimes even moment by moment. Even such clear distinctions as that between comedy and drama should be treated with reserve: in important ways, there are no comic and no serious roles in Shakespeare. Hamlet or Prince Hal, Romeo or Juliet all need to raise laughter and act the fool, drawing on skills that are sometimes considered to be appropriate to comedy. Lady Macbeth and Macbeth are deeply involved in a terrible action, but their minds move with swiftness and fantasy, so they play with words, very like witty persons in a comedy. In all Shakespeare's roles, villain or hero, lover or fool, an actor must be ready to respond outside conventional limitations.

When Shakespeare's Prince Hamlet tried to instruct the players who arrived in the court of Elsinore, he was concerned with their technique and their attention to the text, but "their special observance," he said, should be with "nature":

> for anything so o'erdone is from the purpose of playing,
> whose end, both at the first and now, was and is to hold, as
> 'twere, the mirror up to nature. . . .
>
>   *(Hamlet*, III.ii.1 ff.)

The key phrase, "hold the mirror up to nature," sounds like a generalized instruction: show everyone what they look like, but in context it is precise. Hamlet is in the process of castigating actors' faults and he continues in the same vein:

> O there be players that I have seen play—and heard others
> praise, and that highly—not to speak it profanely, that, nei-
> ther having th'accent of Christians, nor the gait of Chris-
> tian, pagan nor man, have so strutted and bellowed that I
> have thought some of Nature's journeymen had made men,
> and not made them well, they imitated humanity so
> abominably.

The actors have to "make men"; they have to be highly skilled craftspersons, not ordinary workmen ("journeymen"). Characters have to move and speak, and function, as we do: they have been individually crafted and must be alive with individuality. Slowly, skillfully, and adventurously, an actor must build an illusion of a living being, one for whom Shakespeare's text is a necessary extension of existence. Hamlet does not speak for Shakespeare, but in creating this character the dramatist wrote with such freedom, precision, and obvious pleasure that he must have drawn more deeply than usual on his own ideas and reactions. Lacking Shakespeare's advice to the players, Hamlet's is a good substitute.

Another Perspective

Neil Freeman

For another perspective on this famous speech, here is Neil Freeman's Folio version of the text with his commentary:

SPEAKE THE SPEECH I PRAY YOU, AS I PRONOUNC'D   3.2.1–45

Background: Just before the playing of the requested "The Murther of Gonzago" (with "some dosen or sixteene lines" added by Hamlet for Claudius's benefit), Hamlet seems to feel the need to instruct the actors in their business (or as the scholars suggest, Shakespeare felt the need to remind *his* own actors of *their* craft, which some of them seem to have neglected).

Style: general address to a small group
Where: somewhere near the great hall of the castle
To Whom: the first player and colleagues (an unspecified number)
# of Lines: 40   **Probable Timing:** 2.00 minutes

Hamlet 1   Speake the Speech I pray you, as I pronounc'd
it to you trippingly on the Tongue : But if you mouth it,
as many of your Players do, I had as live the Town-Cryer
had spoke my Lines : Nor do not saw the Ayre too much [ ]
your hand thus, but use all gently ; for in the verie Torrent,
Tempest, and (as I may say) the Whirle-winde of [ ]
Passion, you must acquire and beget a Temperance that
may give it Smoothnesse .

2   O it offends mee to the Soule, to
[see] a robustious Pery-wig-pated Fellow teare a Passion to tatters, to verie ragges, to split the eares of the
Groundlings : who (for the most part) are capeable of
nothing, but inexplicable dumbe shewes, & noise : I [could]
have such a Fellow whipt for o're-doing Termagant : it
out-Herod's Herod .

3   Pray you avoid it .

_____

4 Be not too tame neyther : but let your owne
Discretion be your Tutor .

5   Sute the Action to the Word,
the Word to the Action, with this speciall observance : That
you [ore-stop] not the modestie of Nature ; for any
thing so [over-done], is [frö] the purpose of Playing, whose
end both at the first and now, was and is, to hold as 'twer

the Mirrour up to Nature ;   to shew Vertue her owne
Feature, Scorne her owne Image, and the verie Age and
Bodie of the Time, his forme and pressure .

6   Now, this
over-done, or come tardie off, though it [make] the unskil-
full laugh, cannot but make the Judicious greeve ; The
censure of the which One, must in your allowance o're-
way a whole Theater of Others .

7   Oh, there bee Players that
I have seene Play, and heard others praise, and that highly
(not to speake it prophanely) that neyther having the accent
of Christians, nor the [gate] of Christian, Pagan, [or Norman],
have so strutted and bellowed, that I have thought some
of Natures Jouerney-men had made men, and not made
them well, they imitated Humanity so abhominably .

---

8   And let those that
play your Clownes, speake no more [then] is set downe for
them .

9   For there be of them, that will themselves laugh,
to set on some quantitie of barren Spectators to laugh
too, though in the meane time, some necessary Question
of the Play be [then] to be considered : that's Villanous, &
shewes a most pittifull Ambition in the Foole that uses it .

10 Go make you readie .

The speech is essentially composed of two parts, Hamlet's instructions to
the actors and his seemingly irrelevant digressions into his own reflections
upon and reactions to what he regards as "bad acting"—and although
commentators offer several contemporary explanations as to why, to sat-
isfy an audience, there still must be a theatrical reason to justify these dis-
tractions. F's orthography shows that whereas the instructions are mainly
intellectual, the sidebars are either emotional or passionate—the need to
release seeming to be very important, perhaps suggesting his distress with

all the bad real-life acting going on around him (Claudius, Rosincrance, Guildensterne, and even Ophelia).

• The importance of the forthcoming event is underscored by there being virtually no unembellished lines throughout the forty-one lines of advice and reminiscence until the very last words, F #10's "Go make you readie."

• The short F #3, "Pray you avoid it," is the other interesting exception, for both it and the very few surround phrases seem to go beyond just advice to the players, but reveal Hamlet's need for outward signs of honorable behavior from all around him:

> . Nor do not saw the Ayre too much [ ] your hand thus, but
>> use all gently ;
> : I could have such a Fellow whipt for o're-doing Termagant :
>> it out-Herod's Herod .
> : that's Villanous, & shewes a most pittifull Ambition in the
>> Foole that uses it .

• The opening advice of "Speake the Speech" is strongly intellectual (F #1, 15/6), only to be broken by strong emotion as he becomes sidetracked into expressing at length what "offends mee to the Soule" (5/9, F #2's first four and a half lines), while the thought of whipping the "Fellow" who offends him becomes totally intellectual (4/0 in F #2's last two surround phrase line and a half)

• After the quiet imploring of the short F #3, as Hamlet returns to his series of instructions his passions return (F #4, 2/2), which he quickly reins in, reestablishing intellectual control (21/9, F #5–6) for the remainder of his instructions

• But once more, as he breaks off into describing bad actors whose performances have offended him, his intellect gives way, this time to passion (8/9, F #7)

• Commentators acknowledge that F #8–9 is a contemporary reference to the "Clownes" of his own company improvising too much, so it's hardly surprising that this moment is first emotional (1/3, F #8), then with the intellectual elaboration (3/1, F #9's first three and a half lines), quickly turning to passion in his final surround phrase denunciation (3/3, F #9's last line and half)

• And after all the verbiage and sidetracks, as the time grows near for the performance that Hamlet hopes will reveal all, at last Hamlet becomes quiet (the unembellished F #10)

BRIEF BACKGROUND TO THE FIRST FOLIO

Neil Freeman

The First Folio

The end of 1623 saw the publication of the justifiably famed First Folio (F1). The single volume, published in a run of approximately one thousand copies at the princely sum of one pound (a tremendous risk, considering that a single play would sell at no more than six pence, one-fortieth of F1's price, and that the annual salary of a schoolmaster was only ten pounds), contained thirty-six plays.

The manuscripts from which each F1 play would be printed came from a variety of sources. Some had already been printed. Some came from the playhouse complete with production details. Some had no theatrical input at all but were handsomely copied out and easy to read. Some were supposedly very messy, complete with first draft scribbles and crossings out. Yet, as Charlton Hinman, the revered dean of First Folio studies, describes F1 in the Introduction to the Norton Facsimile:

> It is of inestimable value for what it is, for what it contains. For here are preserved the masterworks of the man universally recognized as our greatest writer; and preserved, as Ben Jonson realized at the time of the original publication, not for an age but for all time.

What Does F1 Represent?

- texts prepared for actors who rehearsed three days for a new play and one day for one already in the repertoire
- written in a style (rhetoric incorporating debate) so different from ours (grammatical) that many modern alterations based on grammar (or poetry) have done remarkable harm to the rhetorical/debate quality of the original text and thus to interpretations of characters
- written for an acting company the core of which steadily grew older, and whose skills and interests changed markedly over twenty years as well as for an audience whose makeup and interests likewise changed as the company grew more experienced

28

The whole is based upon supposedly the best documents available at the time, collected by men closest to Shakespeare throughout his career, and brought to a single printing house whose errors are now widely understood—far more than those of some of the printing houses that produced the original quartos.

The Key Question

What text have you been working with—a good modern text or an "original" text, that is, a copy of one of the first printings of the play?

If it's a modern text, no matter how well edited, despite all the learned information offered, it's not surprising that you feel somewhat at a loss, for there is a huge difference between the original printings (the First Folio and the individual quartos) and any text prepared after 1700 right up to the most modern of editions. All the post-1700 texts have been tidied up for the modern reader to ingest silently, revamped according to the rules of correct grammar, syntax, and poetry. However, the "originals" were prepared for actors speaking aloud, playing characters often in a great deal of emotional and/or intellectual stress, and were set down on paper according to the very flexible rules of rhetoric and a seemingly very cavalier attitude toward the rules of grammar, and syntax, and spelling, and capitalization, and even poetry.

Unfortunately, because of the grammatical and syntactical standardization in place by the early 1700s, many of the quirks and oddities of the original also have been dismissed as "accidental"—usually as compositor error either in deciphering the original manuscript, falling prey to their own particular idosyncracies, or not having calculated correctly the amount of space needed to set the text. Modern texts dismiss the possibility that these very quirks and oddities may be by Shakespeare, hearing his characters in as much difficulty as poor Peter Quince is in *A Midsummer Night's Dream* (when he, as the Prologue, terrified and struck down by stage fright, makes a huge grammatical hash in introducing his play "Pyramus and Thisbe" before the aristocracy, whose acceptance or rejection can make or break him):

> If we offend, it is with our good will.
> That you should think, we come not to offend,
> But with good will.

To show our simple skill,

That is the true beginning of our end .

Consider then, we come but in despite.

We do not come, as minding to content you ,

Our true intent is.

All for your delight

We are not here.

That you should here repent you,

The Actors are at hand; and by their show,

You shall know all, that you are like to know.

(*A Midsummer Night's Dream*)

In many other cases in the complete works what was originally printed is equally "peculiar," but, unlike Peter Quince, these peculiarities are usually regularized by most modern texts.

Most of these "peculiarities" resulted from Shakespeare setting down for his actors the stresses, trials, and tribulations the characters are experiencing as they think and speak, and thus are theatrical gold dust for the actor, director, scholar, teacher, and general reader alike.

The First Essential Difference between the Two Texts: Thinking

A **modern** text can show:

- the story line
- your character's conflict with the world at large
- your character's conflict with certain individuals within that world

but because of the very way an "original" text was set, it can show you all this plus one key extra, the very thing that makes big speeches what they are:

- the conflict within the character

WHY?

Any good playwright writes about characters in stressful situations who are often in a state of conflict, not only with the world around them and the people in that world, but also within themselves. And you probably know from personal experience that when these conflicts occur, people do not necessarily utter the most perfect of grammatical/poetic/syntactic statements, phrases, or sentences. Joy and delight, pain and sorrow often come sweeping through in the way things are said, in the incoherence of the phrases, the running together of normally disassociated ideas, and even in the sounds of the words themselves.

The tremendous advantage of the period in which Shakespeare was setting his plays down on paper and how they first appeared in print was that when characters were rational and in control of self and situation, their phrasing and sentences (and poetic structure) would appear to be quite normal even to a modern eye—but when things were going wrong, these sentences and phrasing (and poetic structure) would become highly erratic. But the Quince-type eccentricities are rarely allowed to stand. Sadly, in tidying, most modern texts usually make the text far too clean, thus setting rationality when none originally existed.

The Second Essential Difference between First Folio and Modern Texts: Speaking, Arguing, Debating

Having discovered what and how you or your character is thinking is only the first stage of the work. You/the character then have to speak aloud, in a society that absolutely loved to speak—and not only speak ideas (content) but to speak entertainingly so as to keep listeners enthralled (and this was especially so when you have little content to offer and have to mask it somehow; think of today's television adverts and political spin doctors as a parallel, and you get the picture). Indeed one of the Elizabethan "how to win an argument" books was very precise about this: George Puttenham, *The Art of English Poesie* (1589).

ELIZABETHAN SCHOOLING

All educated classes could debate/argue at the drop of a hat, for both boys (in "petty-schools") and girls (by books and tutors) were trained in what was known overall as the art of rhetoric, which itself was split into three parts:

- First, how to distinguish the real from false appearances/outward show (think of the three caskets in *The Merchant of Venice* in which the language on the gold and silver caskets enticingly, and deceptively, seems to offer hopes of great personal rewards that are dashed when the language is carefully explored, whereas once the apparent threat on the lead casket is carefully analyzed, the reward therein is the greatest that could be hoped for).

- Second, how to frame your argument on one of "three great grounds": honor/morality; justice/legality; and, when all else fails, expedience/ practicality.
- Third, how to order and phrase your argument so winsomely that your audience will vote for you no matter how good the opposition—and there were well over two hundred rules and variations by which winning could be achieved, all of which had to be assimilated before a child's education was considered over and done with.

Thinking on Your Feet: That Is, The Quick, Deft, Rapid Modification of Each Tiny Thought

The Elizabethan—therefore, your character, and therefore, you—was also trained to explore and modify thoughts as they spoke—never would you see a sentence in its entirety and have it perfectly worked out in your mind before you spoke (unless it was a deliberately written, formal public declaration, as with the Officer of the Court in *The Winter's Tale*, reading the charges against Hermione). Thus, after uttering your very first phrase, you might expand it, or modify it, deny it, change it, and so on throughout the whole sentence and speech.

From the poet Samuel Taylor Coleridge, there is a wonderful description of how Shakespeare put thoughts together like "a serpent twisting and untwisting in its own strength," that is, with one thought springing out of the one previous. Treat each new phrase as a fresh unraveling of the serpent's coil. What is discovered (and therefore said) is only revealed as the old coil/phrase disappears, revealing a new coil in its place. The new coil is the new thought. The old coil moves/disappears because the previous phrase is finished with as soon as it is spoken.

Modern Application

It is very rarely that we speak dispassionately in our "real" lives. After all, thoughts give rise to feelings, feelings give rise to thoughts, and we usually speak both together—unless

1. we're trying very hard for some reason to control ourselves and not give ourselves away;

2. or the volcano of emotions within us is so strong that we cannot control ourselves, and feelings swamp thoughts;

3. and sometimes whether deliberately or unconsciously, we color words according to our feelings; the humanity behind the words so revealed is instantly understandable.

How the Original Texts Naturally Enhance/Underscore This Control or Release

The amazing thing about the way all Elizabethan/early Jacobean texts were first set down (the term used to describe the printed words on the page being "orthography"), is that it was flexible, allowing for such variations to be automatically set down without fear of grammatical repercussion.

So if Shakespeare heard Juliet's Nurse working hard to try to convince Juliet that the Prince's nephew Juliet is being forced to (bigamously) marry, instead of setting the everyday normal

> O he's a lovely gentleman

which the modern texts HAVE to set, the first printings were permitted to set

> O hee's a Lovely Gentleman

suggesting that something might be going on inside the Nurse that causes her to release such excessive energy.

Be Careful

This needs to be stressed very carefully: the orthography doesn't dictate to you/force you to accept exactly what it means. The orthography simply suggests that you might want to explore this moment further or more deeply.

In other words, simply because of the flexibility with which the Elizabethans/Shakespeare could set down on paper what they heard in their minds or wanted their listeners to hear, in addition to all the modern acting necessities of character—situation, objective, intention, action, and tactics—the original Shakespeare texts offer pointers to where feelings (either emotional or intellectual, or when combined together as passion, both) are also evident.

Summary

BASIC APPROACH TO FIRST FOLIO SPEECHES ON THE FOLLOWING PAGES:

1. First, use the modern version shown first. By doing so you can discover:

- the basic plot line of what's happening to the character
- the first set of conflicts/obstacles impinging on the character as a result of the situation or actions of other characters
- the supposed grammatical and poetical correctnesses of the speech

2. Then you can explore:

- any acting techniques you'd apply to any modern soliloquy, including establishing for the character
- the given circumstances of the scene
- their outward state of being (who they are sociologically, etc.)
- their intentions and objectives
- the resultant action and tactics they decide to pursue

3. When this is complete, consult the First Folio version of the text. This will help you discover and explore:

- the precise thinking and debating process so essential to an understanding of any Shakespeare text
- the moments when the text is *not* grammatically or poetically as correct as the modern texts would have you believe, which will in turn help you recognize the moments of conflict and struggle stemming from within the character itself
- the sense of fun and enjoyment Shakespeare's language nearly always offers you no matter how dire the situation

Should you wish to further explore even more the differences between the two texts, the commentary that follows discusses how the First Folio has been changed and what those alterations might mean for the human arc of the speech.

Notes on How the First Folio Speeches Are Set Up

Each of the scenes that follow consists of the modern text with commentary, as well as select speeches from the First Folio, which will include the background on the speech and other information including number of lines, approximate timing, and who is addressed.

PROBABLE TIMING: Shown on the page before the speech begins. 0.45 = a forty-five-second speech

Symbols & Abbreviations in the Commentary and Text

F: the First Folio

mt.: modern texts

F # followed by a number: the number of the sentence under discussion in the First Folio version of the speech; thus F #7 would refer to the seventh sentence

mt. # followed by a number: the number of the sentence under discussion in the modern text version of the speech, thus mt. #5 would refer to the fifth sentence

/# (e.g., 3/7): the first number refers to the number of capital letters in the passage under discussion; the second refers to the number of long spellings therein

/ within a quotation from the speech, the "/" symbol indicates where one verse line ends and a fresh one starts

[ ] : set around words in both texts when F1 sets one word, mt another

{ } : some minor alteration has been made, in a speech built up, where a word or phrase will be changed, added, or removed

{†} : this symbol shows where a sizable part of the text is omitted

Terms Found in the Commentary

OVERALL

1. **orthography**: the capitalization, spellings, punctuation of the First Folio

SIGNS OF IMPORTANT DISCOVERIES/ARGUMENTS WITHIN A FIRST FOLIO SPEECH

2. **major punctuation**: colons and semicolons: since the Shakespeare texts are based so much on the art of debate and argument, the importance of F1's major punctuation must not be underestimated, for both the semicolon (;) and colon (:) mark a moment of importance for the character, either for itself, as a moment of discovery or revelation, or as a

key point in a discussion, argument, or debate that it wishes to impress upon other characters onstage.

As a rule of thumb:

a. the more frequent colon (:) suggests that whatever the power of the point discovered or argued, the character is not sidetracked and can continue with the argument—as such, the colon can be regarded as a **logical** connection

b. the far less frequent semicolon (;) suggests that because of the power inherent in the point discovered or argued, the character is sidetracked and momentarily loses the argument and falls back into itself or can only continue the argument with great difficulty—as such, the semicolon should be regarded as an **emotional** connection

3. **surround phrases**: phrase(s) surrounded by major punctuation, or a combination of major punctuation and the end or beginning of a sentence: thus these phrases seem to be of special importance for both character and speech, well worth exploring as key to the argument made and/or emotions released

A LOOSE RULE OF THUMB TO THE THINKING PROCESS OF A FIRST FOLIO CHARACTER

1. mental discipline/**intellect**: a section where capitals dominate suggests that the intellectual reasoning behind what is being spoken or discovered is of more concern than the personal response beneath it

2. feelings/**emotions**: a section where long spellings dominate suggests that the personal response to what is being spoken or discovered is of more concern than the intellectual reasoning behind it

3. **passion**: a section where both long spellings and capitals are present in almost equal proportions suggests that mind and emotion/feelings are inseparable, and thus the character is speaking passionately

SIGNS OF LESS THAN GRAMMATICAL THINKING WITHIN A FIRST FOLIO SPEECH

1. **onrush**: sometimes thoughts are coming so fast that several topics are joined together as one long sentence, suggesting that the F character's mind is working very quickly, or that his/her emotional state is causing some concern. Most modern texts split such a sentence into several grammatically correct parts (the opening speech of *As You Like It* is a

fine example, where F's long eighteen-line opening sentence is split into six), while the modern texts' resetting may be syntactically correct, the F moment is nowhere near as calm as the revisions suggest.

2. **fastlink**: sometimes F shows thoughts moving so quickly for a character that the connecting punctuation between disparate topics is merely a comma, suggesting that there is virtually no pause in springing from one idea to the next. Unfortunately, most modern texts rarely allow this to stand, instead replacing the obviously disturbed comma with a grammatical period, once more creating calm that it seems the original texts never intended to show.

FIRST FOLIO SIGNS OF WHEN VERBAL GAME PLAYING HAS TO STOP

1. **nonembellished**: a section with neither capitals nor long spellings suggests that what is being discovered or spoken is so important to the character that there is no time to guss it up with vocal or mental excesses: an unusual moment of self-control.

2. **short sentence**: coming out of a society where debate was second nature, many of Shakespeare's characters speak in long sentences in which ideas are stated, explored, redefined, and summarized, all before moving on to the next idea in the argument, discovery, or debate. The longer sentence is the sign of a rhetorically trained mind used to public speaking (oratory), but at times an idea or discovery is so startling or inevitable that length is either unnecessary or impossible to maintain: hence the occasional very important short sentence suggests that there is no time for the niceties of oratorical adornment with which to sugar the pill—verbal games are at an end, and now the basic core of the issue must be faced.

3. **monosyllabic**: with English being composed of two strands, the polysyllabic (stemming from French, Italian, Latin, and Greek), and the monosyllabic (from the Anglo-Saxon), each strand has two distinct functions: the polysyllabic words are often used when there is time for fanciful elaboration and rich description (which could be described as "excessive rhetoric") while the monosyllabic occur when, literally, there is no other way of putting a basic question or comment: Juliet's "Do you love me? I know thou wilt say aye" is a classic example of both monosyllables and non-embellishment. With monosyllables, only the naked truth is being spoken; nothing is hidden.

ROMEO AND JULIET

Act II, Scene ii

ROMEO and JULIET

In disguise among a party of young men, Romeo has gate-crashed a festive ball given by the Capulets, his family's most hated enemies. All other guests have gone and in the darkness Romeo has given his friends the slip, climbed over the garden wall and stands, now, hoping to catch sight of the girl with whom he had danced. They had talked together and kissed. Romeo is obsessed by Juliet, as previously he had been with Rosaline, only more completely and still more devotedly.

For Juliet, the meeting has been her first experience of love, and now she leans out of her bedroom window, or comes out onto its balcony, to collect her thoughts and enjoy new and thronging sensations.

Throughout the scene the lovers remain at a distance from each other (although by stretching they may just touch fingers), and both are in danger of discovery.

The noise offstage at line 135 and the Nurse's cries can be supplied easily, but it would be sufficient for an audience if Juliet were to imagine that she hears these disturbances.

❧

Enter ROMEO.

ROMEO

He jests at scars that never felt a wound.

Enter JULIET *at a window, above.*

But soft! What light through yonder window breaks?

It is the East, and Juliet is the sun!

Arise, fair sun, and kill the envious moon

2 **soft** stop

38

Who is already sick and pale with grief   5

That thou her maid art far more fair than she.

Be not her maid since she is envious:

Her vestal livery is but sick and green

And none but fools do wear it. Cast it off.

It is my lady! O it is my love!   10

O that she knew she were!

She speaks yet she says nothing. What of that?

Her eye discourses; I will answer it.

I am too bold; 'tis not to me she speaks.

Two of the fairest stars in all the heaven,   15

Having some business, do entreat her eyes

To twinkle in their spheres till they return.

What if her eyes were there, they in her head?

The brightness of her cheek would shame those stars

As daylight doth a lamp; her eyes in heaven   20

Would through the airy region stream so bright

That birds would sing and think it were not night.

See how she leans her cheek upon her hand!

O that I were a glove upon that hand

That I might touch that cheek!

JULIET   Ay me!

ROMEO   She speaks.   25

O speak again bright angel, for thou art

As glorious to this night, being o'er my head,

As is a winged messenger of heaven

Unto the white-upturnèd wond'ring eyes

Of mortals that fall back to gaze on him   30

---

6 **maid** (virgins were the maids of
   Diana, the moon goddess)
8 **vestal** virgin **green** anemic (wordplay on the motley green dress of
   court fools)

13 **discourses** speaks
17 **spheres** orbits
21 **region** (of the sky)
29 **white-upturned** looking up, so that
   the whites only are seen on earth

When he bestrides the lazy puffing clouds

And sails upon the bosom of the air.

JULIET

O Romeo, Romeo! Wherefore art thou Romeo?

Deny thy father and refuse thy name

Or, if thou wilt not, be but sworn my love   35

And I'll no longer be a Capulet.

ROMEO *(Aside.)*

Shall I hear more or shall I speak at this?

JULIET

'Tis but thy name that is my enemy.

Thou art thyself, though not a Montague.

What's a Montague? It is nor hand, nor foot,   40

Nor arm, nor face, nor any other part

Belonging to a man. O be some other name!

What's in a name? That which we call a rose

By any other word would smell as sweet.

So Romeo would, were he not Romeo called,   45

Retain that dear perfection which he owes

Without that title. Romeo doff thy name,

And for thy name which is no part of thee

Take all myself.

ROMEO   I take thee at thy word.

Call me but love and I'll be new baptized;   50

Henceforth I never will be Romeo.

JULIET

What man art thou that, thus bescreened in night,

So stumblest on my counsel?

---

34 **Deny** disown **refuse** renounce   48 **for** In exchange for
39 **though not** even if you were not   49 **at thy word** at once/as you offer
46 **owes** owns   yourself
47 **doff** put off, thrust aside   53 **counsel** secret, private thoughts

ROMEO   By a name

    I know not how to tell thee who I am.

    My name, dear saint, is hateful to myself   55

    Because it is an enemy to thee.

    Had I it written, I would tear the word.

JULIET

    My ears have yet not drunk a hundred words

    Of thy tongue's uttering yet I know the sound.

    Art thou not Romeo and a Montague?   60

ROMEO

    Neither, fair maid, if either thee dislike.

JULIET

    How camest thou hither, tell me, and wherefore?

    The orchard walls are high and hard to climb

    And the place death, considering who thou art,

    If any of my kinsmen find thee here.   65

ROMEO

    With love's light wings did I o'erperch these walls

    For stony limits cannot hold love out,

    And what love can do that dares love attempt,

    Therefore thy kinsmen are no stop to me.

JULIET

    If they do see thee, they will murder thee.   70

ROMEO

    Alack, there lies more peril in thine eye

    Than twenty of their swords! Look thou but sweet

    And I am proof against their enmity.

JULIET

    I would not for the world they saw thee here.

---

61 **dislike** displease   66 **o'erperch** surmount

62 **wherefore** why   73 **proof against** invulnerable to

ROMEO

> I have night's cloak to hide me from their eyes,   75
> And but thou love me, let them find me here.
> My life were better ended by their hate
> Than death prorogued, wanting of thy love.

JULIET

> By whose direction found'st thou out this place?

ROMEO

> By Love that first did prompt me to inquire: 80
> He lent me counsel and I lent him eyes.
> I am no pilot, yet wert thou as far
> As that vast shore washed with the farthest sea,
> I should adventure for such merchandise.

JULIET

> Thou knowest the mask of night is on my face   85
> Else would a maiden blush bepaint my cheek
> For that which thou hast heard me speak tonight.
> Fain would I dwell on form-fain, fain deny
> What I have spoke. But farewell compliment!
> Dost thou love me? I know thou wilt say "Ay"   90
> And I will take thy word. Yet if thou swear'st,
> Thou mayst prove false. At lovers' perjuries,
> They say Jove laughs. O gentle Romeo,
> If thou dost love, pronounce it faithfully.
> Or if thou thinkest I am too quickly won,   95
> I'll frown and be perverse and say thee nay
> So thou wilt woo; but else, not for the world.

76 **but** if only
78 **prorogued** deferred
81 **I . . . eyes** (because Love is blind-folded)
83 **that . . . sea** (alluding to the journey toward Death's kingdom)
84 **adventure** risk all/journey

88 **Fain** gladly
dwell on form keep within limits of conventional behavior
89 **compliment** etiquette
94 **pronounce** declare
97 **So** if only

In truth, fair Montague, I am too fond

And therefore thou mayst think my havior light,

But trust me, gentleman, I'll prove more true   100

Than those that have more cunning to be strange.

I should have been more strange, I must confess,

But that thou overheard'st, ere I was ware,

My truelove passion. Therefore pardon me

And not impute this yielding to light love   105

Which the dark night hath so discovered.

ROMEO

Lady, by yonder blessèd moon I vow,

That tips with silver all these fruit-tree tops-

JULIET

O swear not by the moon, th' inconstant moon

That monthly changes in her circled orb,   110

Lest that thy love prove likewise variable.

ROMEO

What shall I swear by?

JULIET   Do not swear at all;

Or if thou wilt, swear by thy gracious self

Which is the god of my idolatry,

And I'll believe thee.

ROMEO   If my heart's dear love—   115

JULIET

Well, do not swear. Although I joy in thee,

I have no joy of this contract tonight.

It is too rash, too unadvised, too sudden,

Too like the lightning which doth cease to be

98 **fond** affectionate/foolish

99 **havior** behavior

light lightheaded, unmodest

101 **strange** distant, reserved

103 **ware** aware

104 **passion** outburst, expression of
   deep feeling

105 **light** easy/wanton

106 **discovered** revealed

117 **contract** exchange of vows

Ere one can say it lightens. Sweet, good night!   120

This bud of love, by summer's ripening breath,

May prove a beauteous flow'r when next we meet.

Good night, good night! As sweet repose and rest

Come to thy heart as that within my breast!

ROMEO

O wilt thou leave me so unsatisfied?   125

JULIET

What satisfaction canst thou have tonight?

ROMEO

The exchange of thy love's faithful vow for mine.

JULIET

I gave thee mine before thou didst request it;

And yet I would it were to give again.

ROMEO

Wouldst thou withdraw it? For what purpose, love?   130

JULIET

But to be frank and give it thee again.

And yet I wish but for the thing I have:

My bounty is as boundless as the sea,

My love as deep; the more I give to thee,

The more I have, for both are infinite.   135

I hear some noise within. Dear love, adieu!

(NURSE calls from within.)

Anon, good nurse! Sweet Montague, be true

Stay but a little, I will come again.   *Exit*

ROMEO

O blessèd, blessèd night! I am afeard,

Being in night, all this is but a dream,   140

124 **as that** as to that heart which is   133 **bounty** kindness/liberty/gift
131 **frank** free, generous   137 **Anon** coming

Too flattering-sweet to be substantial.

Enter JULIET again.

JULIET

Three words, dear Romeo, and good night indeed.

If that thy bent of love be honorable,

Thy purpose marriage, send me word tomorrow,

By one that I'll procure to come to thee,   145

Where and what time thou wilt perform the rite

And all my fortunes at thy foot I'll lay

And follow thee my lord throughout the world.

(NURSE Within. Madam!)

JULIET

I come anon.—But if thou meanest not well,

I do beseech thee—

(NURSE Within. Madam!)

JULIET   By and by I come.-   150

To cease thy strife and leave me to my grief.

Tomorrow will I send.

ROMEO   So thrive my soul—

JULIET

A thousand times good night!   *Exit.*

ROMEO

A thousand times the worse, to want thy light!

Love goes toward love as schoolboys from their books   155

But love from love, toward school with heavy looks.

141 **substantial** real	150 **By and by** immediately
143 **bent** aim, force (as of a bent bow)	151 **strife** striving
145 **procure** arrange	152 **So . . . soul** as I hope to be saved
147 **fortunes** possessions/fortune	154 **want** lack
149 **anon** at once	

Enter JULIET again.

JULIET

    Hist! Romeo, hist! O for a falc'ner's voice

    To lure this tassel gentle back again!

    Bondage is hoarse and may not speak aloud,

    Else would I tear the cave where Echo lies   160

    And make her airy tongue more hoarse than mine

    With repetition of "My Romeo!"

ROMEO

    It is my soul that calls upon my name.

    How silver-sweet sound lovers' tongues by night,

    like softest music to attending ears!   165

JULIET

    Romeo!

ROMEO   My sweet?

JULIET   What o'clock tomorrow

    Shall I send to thee?

ROMEO   By the hour of nine.

JULIET

    I will not fail. 'Tis twenty years till then.

    I have forgot why I did call thee back.

ROMEO

    Let me stand here till thou remember it.   170

JULIET

    I shall forget, to have thee still stand there,

    Rememb'ring how I love thy company.

---

158 **lure** recall (a term of falconry)
    tassel gentle male peregrine
    falcon
159 **Bondage is hoarse** I am watched
    and can only whisper

160 **tear the cave** pierce the air
    Echo (a nymph who pined for Narcis-
    sus until only her voice was left)
165 **attending** attentive
171 **still** always

ROMEO

And I'll still stay to have thee still forget,

Forgetting any other home but this.

JULIET

'Tis almost morning: I would have thee gone   175

And yet no farther than a wanton's bird,

That lets it hop a little from his hand

Like a poor prisoner in his twisted gyves,

And with a silken thread plucks it back again,

So loving-jealous of his liberty.   180

ROMEO

I would I were thy bird.

JULIET   Sweet, so would I,

Yet I should kill thee with much cherishing.

Good night, good night! Parting is such sweet sorrow

That I shall say good night till it be morrow.   *Exit.*

ROMEO

Sleep dwell upon thine eyes, peace in thy breast!   185

Would I were sleep and peace, so sweet to rest!

Hence will I to my ghostly friar's close cell,

His help to crave and my dear hap to tell.   *Exit.*

176 **wanton's** playful child's
178 **gyves** fetters
179 **thread** (tied to its leg)
184 **morrow** morning

187 **ghostly** spiritual
close secluded, private
188 **dear hap** good fortune

ᘓᘔ

Rehearsing the Scene

Romeo's first line is said either to his friends who have laughed at him for being in love, or to himself, thoughts of Juliet making everything else seem trivial.

Before Juliet speaks a word, it should be clear that she is wrapped up in her first love. Romeo's opening speech supplies some stage directions for her, but these are not all that is required: the actress has to ensure that every movement and breath comes from a continuous and ardent involvement in a totally new experience.

Some short verse lines (11.42, 153) suggest silences during this scene, but there can be many more, especially when a verse line concludes with a full stop. Full stops in the middle of lines should not be allowed to break the strong drive forward provided by the full lines of verse; they indicate no more than a slight pause, for the start of a new idea and new breath.

Both actors need to keep their thoughts racing and their sensations exceptionally rich and exploratory in order to provide the motivations for speaking so many words. Imaginary sights have to be created in their minds. Romeo envisions the whole night sky and the next moment seems to hear birds singing endlessly (11.20–22); then his thoughts are of angels, revelation, worshipping mortals, and levitation (11.26–32). Juliet is more practical in her thoughts, until Romeo's oath makes her think of the "inconstant moon" (1.109); and then her fear, or her urgent desire to understand and so possess new experiences, must be checked by amazement, impatience, sheer pleasure; toward the end of the scene her mind is alive with images of the hunt, imprisonment, and cries for help.

Romeo and Juliet are both so excited that even their most serious thoughts are enlivened by a keen sense of humor, as if they find their wonder almost absurd, or as if they have to laugh to avoid crying or to avoid being simply speechless. For example, Romeo seeing Juliet rest her face in her hand suddenly wants to be a glove upon that hand (1.24); is this self-mockery, making light of an unfulfilled desire to be close to Juliet, or an excited recognition of sexual drive and physical awareness?

They also have a sharp sense of immediate reality. Short sentences represent thoughts that stab their consciousness: Romeo's "But soft . . . Cast it off. . . . it is my Lady . . . What of that? . . . She speaks"; and Juliet's thoughts, more weighty than his, "Dost thou love me? . . . Do not swear at all. . . . Well, do not swear. . . . Romeo . . . I will not fail." However, Juliet's first encounters with Romeo are speeches that run fully and strongly within single verse lines (see 11.60, 62, 70, 74, and 79).

Their struggle toward mutual understanding and security comes to a momentary crisis with Romeo's line "O wilt thou leave me so unsatisfied?" (1.125). This is developed further after a momentary fear of being discovered, by Juliet, with "If that thy bent of love be honorable" (1.143). Still, it becomes increasingly obvious that they must for now part immediately. Yet the two lovers instinctively hold back (see 11.169–74): shared silences can now be lengthy or brief; movement almost nil, or nervous and almost incessant.

First Folio Speeches

For another perspective, following are speeches from the scene from the First Folio with commentary by Neil Freeman drawn from the *Once More Unto the Speech* series.

ROMEO   HE JEASTS AT SCARRES THAT NEVER FELT A WOUND,

Background: Following the first meeting with Juliet, and the kissing of her mouth, twice, Romeo attempts to elude his friends: accidentally coming close to the upper-level balcony guarding Juliet's bedroom (though he doesn't realize it yet), he has been forced to hide from the unwarranted and incredibly raunchy intrusion of Mercutio and the somewhat embarrassed and concerned Benvolio. The following is Romeo's immediate response to their exit.

Style: solo

Where: outside, close to the balcony leading to Juliet's bedroom

To Whom: self, the audience, and Juliet on the balcony (but not so that she can hear)

# of Lines: 32   **Probable Timing:** 1.35 minutes

Romeo

1   He jeasts at Scarres that never felt a wound,
     But soft, what light through yonder window breaks ?

2   It is the East, and Juliet is the Sunne,
     Arise faire Sun and kill the envious Moone,
     Who is already sicke and pale with griefe,
     That thou her Maid art far more faire [then] she :
     Be not her Maid since she is envious,
     Her Vestal livery is but sicke and greene,

And none but fooles do weare it, cast it off :
It is my Lady, O it is my Love, O that she knew she were,
She speakes, yet she sayes nothing, what of that ?

3   Her eye discourses, I will answere it :
     I am too bold 'tis not to me she speakes :
     Two of the fairest starres in all the Heaven,
     Having some businesse do entreat her eyes,
     To twinckle in their Spheres till they returne .

4   What if her eyes were there, they in her head,
     The brightnesse of her cheeke would shame those starres,
     As day-light doth a Lampe, her [eye] in heaven,
     Would through the ayrie Region streame so bright,
     That Birds would sing, and thinke it were not night :
     See how she leanes her cheeke upon her hand .

5   O that I were a Glove upon that hand,
     That I might touch that cheeke .

6   She speakes .

7   Oh speake againe bright Angell, for thou art
     As glorious to this night being ore my head,
     As is a winged messenger of heaven
     Unto the white upturned wondring eyes
     Of mortalls that fall backe to gaze on him,
     When he bestrides the lazie puffing Cloudes,
     And sailes upon the bosome of the ayre .

     F's often onrushed seven sentences and the very long penultimate line
of F #2 present the pattern of a lovestruck young man far more effectively
than the seventeen sentences and much more regular setting of mt. #6–7
that most modern texts offer.
     • The opening onrush of F #1, connecting the two lines via a fast link
and highly ungrammatical comma seems to suggest that with the light

suddenly appearing, Romeo may be afraid that his somewhat passionate denigration of Mercutio and Benvolio (2/1, F #1's first line) might have led to his being discovered, especially since the second unembellished line is obviously very quiet.

• Once he realizes the light comes from Juliet's room (and he perhaps sees her), so F #2's first five lines are passionate (6/5) while the end of the sentence, with the exception of the extra-long line discussed immediately below, is highly emotional (2/6), as are F #3's first two surround phrase lines pointing to his desire/yet inability to act:

> . Her eye discourses, I will answere it : /
> I am too bold 'tis not to me she speakes :

• The strongly factual F and Q sixteen-syllable line "It is my Lady, O it is my Love, O that she knew she were," (4/0) suggests an enormous release as he declares his love, at least to himself: most modern texts reset it as shown, reducing the outburst to a regular line followed by a short one of six syllables, implying a pause that was never originally intended.

• While still emotional, his eight-line dwelling on her eyes as "Two of the fairest starres in all the Heaven," allows some intellect to creep back in (5/10, the last three lines of F #3 plus F #4's first five lines), especially after the wonderfully unembellished F #4 start to his fanciful flight of imagination "What if her eyes were there," (i.e., in the Heavens) "they in her head."

• The desire to touch her and hear her speak "againe" releases even more emotion in him (2/8, the last line of F #4, all of F #5, and the extremely short #6, itself a wonderful giveaway as to his besottedness, and the first line of F #7).

• Quite charmingly, the praise of her glory as a "bright Angell" becomes wonderfully quiet and unembellished for three lines (as if the image is almost too much for him to speak) until the final three-line description of "mortalls" who gaze on her as a "winged messenger of heaven" releases his emotions very fully once more (1/6).

JULIET   O ROMEO, ROMEO, WHEREFORE ART THOU ROMEO ?

Background: Thinking she is alone, Juliet reveals that she has been as moved by the first meeting with Romeo as he.

Style: solo

Where: on the balcony leading to her bedroom

To Whom: self and the audience, not knowing Romeo can hear every-
        thing she says

# of Lines: 15   **Probable Timing:** 0.50 minutes

Juliet

1   O Romeo, Romeo, wherefore art thou Romeo ?

2   Denie thy Father and refuse thy name :
    Or if thou wilt not, be but sworne my Love,
    And Ile no longer be a Capulet .

─────────────────────────

3   'Tis but thy name that is my Enemy :
    Thou art thy selfe, though not a [Mountague],
    What's [Mountague] ? it is nor hand nor foote,
    Nor arme, nor face,[1] [O be some other name
    Belonging to a man] .

4   [What] ? in a [names][2] that which we call a Rose,
    By any other word would smell as sweete,
    So Romeo would, were he not Romeo cal'd,
    Retaine that deare perfection which he owes,
    Without that title Romeo,[3] doffe thy name,
    And for thy name which is no part of thee,
    Take all my selfe .

─────────

1   This is the text as set in Q2–4/Ff: however, most modern texts
i) add a phrase from Q1, "nor any other part," and then follow it with ii)
"Belonging to a man," iii) thus placing "O be some other name" last: the
two lines thus read, "Nor arme, nor face, nor any other part/Belonging to
a man. O be some other name."

2   Q2–4/F2/most modern texts = "What's in a name?" (adding
Q1's question mark), F1 = "What? in a names."

3   F1–3 = "Without that title Romeo, doffe thy name,": F4/modern
texts strengthen her request, setting major punctuation before "Romeo,"
viz. "Without that title; Romeo, doffe thy name," (Q2 = ", Romeo, doffe
thy name").

While the first two sentences match in structure, F's onrush (modern texts resetting F #3 as four sentences and F #4 as three) suggests that at the end of F/mt. #2 Juliet suddenly finds a clever verbal way to get out of the dilemma, and the excitement of the discovery causes her to lose some control—and this would seem to be supported by F's peculiar verbal ending to F#3 (mt. #5), most modern texts preferring to set the second quarto version of the text as shown.

• The depth of the dilemma is established straightaway by the opening short intellectual F #1 (3/0), and the first improbable solution is emphasized by being set as a surround phrase " . Denie thy Father and refuse thy name : "

• … while the solution is also expressed as a surround phrase " . 'Tis but thy name that is my Enemy : "

• To this point the speech is almost totally intellectual (7/1 F #1–2, and the first line of F #3), and then, with her onrushed expanding on their way out of the problem "Thou art thy selfe, though not a Mountague," Juliet becomes emotionally passionate (3/5, the three and a half lines ending F #3).

• After the unembellished opening F #4, "What? in a names"—perhaps reinforcing the solution (F only phrasing), she becomes intellectual once more as she equates Romeo with "perfection" (4/2 F #4's next four lines), ending with a final emotional two-line offer concluding with "Take all my selfe." (0/2)

JULIET   THOU KNOWEST THE MASKE OF NIGHT IS ON MY FACE,

Background: Having heard Juliet's closest secrets (prior speech) Romeo has sprung from his hiding place, declaring his love, initially giving Juliet a great shock, since initially she can't see him and has no idea who is being so passionate. Once she discovers who it is, and that he is here because it is "Love that first did prompt me to enquire," she unequivocally confesses her (somewhat mixed) feelings.

Style: as part of a two-handed scene

Where: on her balcony

To Whom: Romeo, below

# of Lines: 22   **Probable Timing:** 1.10 minutes

Juliet

1   Thou knowest the maske of night is on my face,

     Else would a Maiden blush bepaint my cheeke,

     For that which thou hast heard me speake to night,

     Faine would I dwell on forme, faine, faine, denie

     What I have spoke, but farewell Complement,

     Doest thou Love [ ]?

2   I know thou wilt say [I],

     And I will take thy word, yet if thou swear'st,

     Thou maiest prove false : at Lovers perjuries

     They say Jove [laught], oh gentle Romeo,

     If thou dost Love, pronounce it faithfully :

     Or if thou thinkest I am too quickly wonne,

     Ile frowne and be perverse, and say thee nay,

     So thou wilt wooe : But else not for the world.

3   In truth faire [Mountague] I am too fond :

     And therefore thou maiest thinke my [behaviour] light,

     But trust me Gentleman, Ile prove more true,

     [Then] those that have [coying] to be strange,

     I should have beene more strange, I must confesse,

     But that thou over heard'st ere I was ware

     My true [Loves] passion, therefore pardon me,

     And not impute this yeelding to light Love,

     Which the darke night hath so discovered.

Unlike the previous passionate speech (13/10 overall) when Juliet was alone and emotions rarely took over, now she is with Romeo. Though the speech again seems overall passionate (11/15), her emotions almost swamp her, at least as the speech starts.

• Hardly surprisingly, Juliet's initial confession starts emotionally (1/7, F #4's first four lines), but an intellectual determination to speak her mind floods F #1's last line (2/0).

• Following her F #2's unembellished opening fears that Romeo "maiest prove false," her explanation that "Jove laught" at "Lovers perjuries" is intellectual (4/1, the two and a half lines between F #2's first two colons), while the suggestion she would play the courting game of nay-saying if it would better his opinion of her becomes emotional once more (1/3, F #3's last three lines save for the final unembellished phrase).

• F#3's confession of being "too fond" becomes very subdued, with only three releases in the first six lines, while the denial that hers is a "light Love" becomes adamantly passionate (2/2 in the last three lines).

• The few unembellished passages very clearly, carefully, and vulnerably point to her concerns: first as to her fears about possible betrayal (opening F #2), heightened further by being monosyllabic:

> I know thou wilt say I,
> And I will take thy word, yet if thou swear'st,
> Thou maiest prove false :

And then the occasional unembellished phrases referring to the depth of her own love are equally telling: "I am too fond"; "Ile prove more true"; "I should have beene more strange . . . /But that thou over heard'st ere I was ware"; and "therefore pardon me"

• And the two surround phrases also point to the strength of her love, the end of F #2 emphasizing she doesn't want to play courting denial games:

> : But else not for the world .

and the opening of F #3:

> . In truth faire Mountague I am too fond :

JULIET   THREE WORDS DEARE ROMEO,

Background: The exchange of love vows completed, they are interrupted by the nurse in the house calling for Juliet. This speech starts after Juliet returns, having briefly exited, presumably to placate the Nurse (unsuccessfully, it seems, since the Nurse interrupts the following at least twice).

Style: as part of a two-handed scene

Where: on her balcony

To Whom: Romeo, below

# of Lines: 11   **Probable Timing:** 0.40 minutes

5

Juliet

1   Three words deare Romeo,
     And goodnight indeed,
     If that thy bent of Love be Honourable,
     Thy purpose marriage, send me word to morrow,
     By one that Ile procure to come to thee,
     Where and what time thou wilt performe the [right],
     And all my Fortunes at thy foote Ile lay,
     And follow thee my Lord throughout the world.
[Within : Madam]

2   I come, anon : but if thou meanest not well,
     I do beseech theee
[Within: Madam]

     (By and by I come—)
     To cease thy strife, and leave me to my griefe,
     To morrow will I send.

3   A thousand times goodnight .

Considering the sometimes excessive releases elsewhere in the play, not just for Juliet but for all the characters, this is a remarkably contained speech (just 4/5 in eleven lines), suggesting Juliet is taking great care in voicing the idea of marriage.
   • Thus the few releases underscore the tenor of the speech, pointing to
   a. first where her heart is so evidently on her sleeve, "deare Romeo" (0/2)
   b. then still to the question of does he mean it, "If that thy bent of Love be Honourable'" (2/1)
   c. then to the idea of marriage itself, for if he will "performe the right" (0/1) ("right" being a lovely double meaning word somewhat diminished by most modern texts' correcting it to the more obvious and simplistic "rite"), then 'all my Fortunes at thy foote Ile lay/And follow thee my Lord' (2/1)
   d. finally requesting that if he does not mean well, he should leave her to her "griefe" (0/1)

ROMEO AND JULIET

Act II, Scene v

JULIET and the NURSE
☙❦❧

Juliet met Romeo for the first time last night when he arrived unexpect-
edly at the annual party given by her parents. She is fourteen years old and
an only child. After dancing together, the stranger and she had talked and
kissed before parting. Later in the garden under her bedroom window,
Romeo declared his love, and Juliet told him to send word saying where
and when they could be married. As they are the sole heirs of two power-
ful families locked in a bitter, dangerous feud, their passion and devotion
require great secrecy.

Juliet has sent her Nurse to receive Romeo's message and is waiting her
return. Probably she is in the garden, on the lookout, and dressed ready to
go to any rendezvous Romeo names.

The Nurse lives for Juliet, both her own child and her husband having
died many years previously. As a servant in the Capulet house, she has
looked after Juliet since birth and enjoys great familiarity with the whole
household. She is proud of her long service.

There is no need for the Nurse's attendant, Peter, to be present; he can
be dealt with as an offstage character.

☙❦❧

JULIET

The clock struck nine when I did send the nurse.

In half an hour she promised to return.

Perchance she cannot meet him. That's not so.

O she is lame! Love's heralds should be thoughts

Which ten times faster glide than the sun's beams   5

Driving back shadows over low'ring hills,

3 **Perchance** perhaps

57

Therefore do nimble-pinioned doves draw Love

And therefore hath the wind-swift Cupid wings.

Now is the sun upon the highmost hill

Of this day's journey and from nine till twelve   10

Is three long hours; yet she is not come.

Had she affections and warm youthful blood,

She would be as swift in motion as a ball;

My words would bandy her to my sweet love

And his to me.   15

But old folks, many feign as they were dead:

Unwieldy, slow, heavy, and pale as lead.

Enter NURSE and PETER.

O God, she comes! O honey Nurse, what news?

Hast thou met with him? Send thy man away.

NURSE

Peter, stay at the gate.   *Exit PETER.*   20

JULIET

Now good sweet Nurse!--O Lord, why lookest thou sad?

Though news be sad, yet tell them merrily;

If good, thou shamest the music of sweet news

By playing it to me with so sour a face.

NURSE

I am aweary, give me leave awhile.   25

Fie, how my bones ache! What a jaunce have I!

JULIET

I would thou hadst my bones and I thy news.

Nay come, I pray thee speak. Good, good Nurse, speak.

---

7 **nimble-pinioned** swift-winged **doves**
  (sacred to Venus, they draw her
  chariot)
8 **Cupid** (the blindfolded son of Venus)
9 **is . . . hill** it is midday

12 **affections** feelings
16 **feign** act, appear
20 **stay . . . gate** wait at the entrance
25 **give me leave** let me alone
26 **jaunce** jaunt, weary journey

NURSE

    Jesu, what haste! Can you not stay awhile?

    Do you not see that I am out of breath?   30

JULIET

    How art thou out of breath when thou hast breath

    To say to me that thou art out of breath?

    The excuse that thou dost make in this delay

    Is longer than the tale thou dost excuse.

    Is thy news good or bad? Answer to that.   35

    Say either and I'll stay the circumstance.

    Let me be satisfied, is't good or bad?

NURSE Well you have made a simple choice; you know

    not how to choose a man. Romeo? No, not he.

    Though his face be better than any man's, yet   40

    his leg excels all men's, and for a hand and a foot,

    and a body, though they be not to be talked on,

    yet they are past compare. He is not the flower of

    courtesy, but I'll warrant him as gentle as a lamb. Go

    thy ways, wench; serve God. What, have you dined   45

    at home?

JULIET

    No, no. But all this did I know before.

    What says he of our marriage? What of that?

NURSE

    Lord, how my head aches! What a head have I!

    It beats as it would fall in twenty pieces.   50

    My back-a t' other side-ah my back, my back!

    Beshrew your heart for sending me about

    To catch my death with jauncing up and down!

---

29 **stay** wait	51 **a** on
36 **stay the circumstance** wait for details	52 **Beshrew** a curse on
38 **simple** foolish	53 **jauncing** traipsing
42 **not . . . talked on** not worth mentioning	

JULIET

    I' faith I am sorry that thou art not well.

    Sweet, sweet, sweet Nurse, tell me, what says my love?   55

NURSE   Your love says, like an honest gentleman, and

    a courteous, and a kind, and a handsome, and I

    warrant a virtuous-where is your mother?

JULIET

    Where is my mother? Why she is within.

    Where should she be? How oddly thou repliest!   60

    "Your love says, like an honest gentleman,

    'Where is your mother?'"

NURSE   O God's Lady dear!

    Are you so hot? Marry come up, I trow.

    Is this the poultice for my aching bones?

    Henceforward do your messages yourself.   65

JULIET

    Here's such a coil! Come, what says Romeo?

NURSE

    Have you got leave to go to shrift today?

JULIET

    I have.

NURSE

    Then hie you hence to Friar Lawrence' cell;

    There stays a husband to make you a wife.   70

    Now comes the wanton blood up in your cheeks;

    They'll be in scarlet straight at any news.

    Hie you to church. I must another way,

    To fetch a ladder by the which your love

---

56 **honest** honorable   66 **coil** fuss

63 **hot** in a passion, angry   67 **shrift** confession

   Marry . . . trow By the Virgin,   69 **Hie** haste

   come off it, I should think   72 **straight** straightway

Must climb a bird's nest soon when it is dark. 75

I am the drudge and toil in your delight,

But you shall bear the burden soon at night.

Go. I'll to dinner. Hie you to the cell.

JULIET

Hie to high fortune! Honest Nurse, farewell. Exeunt.

75 **bird's nest** i.e., Juliet's room (**bird** = maiden)

76 **in** for

77 **bear the burden** do the work/bear the weight of your lover

CERD

Rehearsing the Scene

Juliet and her nurse could hardly be closer to each other, knowing each other intimately. While Juliet is "hot" to get on with her life and her new love, the Nurse will suffer a real loss in Juliet's departure. Juliet is only fourteen years old, and the nurse continues to treat the future bride like a child.

Much depends on how confident Juliet is at the beginning of the scene, how secure in comparing her lovethoughts to the "sun's beams" (1.5). How aware is she of the uncertainties of "nimble-pinioned" birds, and of blind Cupid?

The Nurse may delay her news deliberately, either for her own pleasure or to test Juliet's seriousness. Or she can be, quite literally, "out of breath" (1.30).

Does Juliet actually rub her Nurse's aching back (see 1.51), or is she too caught up in her own thoughts and feelings to be able to respond? At what point does she shift from demanding the news to cajoling it out of her faithful Nurse? Perhaps the Nurse gets full attention by her account of Romeo's physical attractions. "Go thy ways, wench" (11.44–45) may follow a pause in which both have become silent, still and happy in the contemplation of Romeo's virtues as a lover; or the Nurse can push ahead without further ado, confident that she is totally in charge, and Juliet is ready to do anything she says.

"Here's such a coil," some dozen lines from the end of the scene, suggests a climax in their talk, whether it occurs instinctively or because it has been engineered. Thereafter Juliet has little to say, but much to realize and enjoy—and, perhaps, to fear. The Nurse alludes now to sexual arousal and adventure with greater openness. Juliet's wordplay on "hie" and "high" can express her quick excitement.

Nurse and Juliet leave in opposite directions, the one in slower tempo into the house, the other, more quickly, in the direction from which the Nurse had entered. Juliet does not stop to thank the Nurse, but she may kiss or hug her before running off.

First Folio Speeches

For another perspective, here is the opening speech from the scene from the First Folio with commentary by Neil Freeman drawn from the *Once More Unto the Speech* series.

Juliet The clocke strook nine, when I did send the Nurse,

Background: Juliet is waiting for the Nurse to return from her meeting with Romeo. Unfortunately, though the Nurse left at nine, she didn't meet Romeo until, as Mercutio brazenly put it, "when the bawdy hand of the Dyall" was "upon the pricke of noone," so she is very, very late.

Style: solo

Where: presumably outside in the grounds of the Capulet residence

To Whom: self, and direct audience address

# of Lines: 19   **Probable Timing:** 1.00 minutes

Juliet

1   The clocke strook nine, when I did send the Nurse,
      In halfe an houre she promised to returne,
      Perchance she cannot meete him : that's not so :
      Oh she is lame, Loves [Herauld] should be thoughts,
      Which ten times faster glides [then] the Sunnes beames,
      Driving backe shadowes over lowring hils .

2   Therefore do nimble Pinion'd Doves draw Love,
      And therefore hath the wind-swift Cupid wings :
      Now is the Sun upon the highmost hill
      Of this daies journey, and from nine till twelve,
      [I] three long houres, yet she is not come .

3   Had she affections and warme youthfull blood,

    She would be as swift in motion as a ball,

    My words would bandy her to my sweete Love,

    And his to me, but old folkes,

    Many faine as they were dead,

    Unwieldie, slow, heavy, and pale as lead .

    Enter Nurse

4   O God she comes, O hony Nurse what newes ?

5   Hast thou met with him ? send thy man away .

Since she has been waiting three hours for the Nurse's return (which was scheduled for two and a half hours ago), the fact that the first three lines are highly emotional (1/6) and end in a surround phrase pushing aside thoughts of doom (" : that's not so : ") is hardly surprising.

• The attempt to justify the Nurse's lateness ("Oh she is lame, . . .") at least adds some intellectual control to the speech (3/6) . . .

• . . . which gains more headway as she dwells on classical love images (4/0, F #2's first two lines), but the untroubled mood doesn't seem to last . . .

• . . . for F #2's last three lines, ending with the monosyllabic unembellished "yet she is not come," becomes much less exuberant (1/1) . . .

• . . . and this quietness (an attempt not to give in to emotion? or a quiet pout perhaps?) continues through the mildly emotional F #3 denigration of "old folkes" (1/3 in six lines).

• However, the enormity of her images' attack are underscored both by:

a. the pauses inherent before voicing the melodramatic exaggeration contained in the two unusual short lines "And his to me, but old folkes,/ Many faine as they were dead" (7/7 syllables, the impact reduced by most modern texts resetting the passage as just one short line followed by one of regular length 4/10 syllables)

b. and the two unembellished lines that if the Nurse were young and had "'affections," "She would be as swift in motion as a ball," and the less than flattering description as Juliet finds her to be "Unwieldie, slow, heavy and pale as lead."

• Yet when the Nurse enters, all control momentarily disappears with F #4's excited intellect of "O God she comes, . . ." (3/0), only to be followed by F #5's two short unembellished surround phrases that end the speech.

ROMEO AND JULIET

Act III, Scene v

LADY CAPULET and JULIET

ය80

Sent by her husband, Lady Capulet enters Juliet's bedroom in the first light of morning. Her task is to persuade her daughter to a quickly arranged marriage with Paris, a young nobleman whom she hardly knows at all. This is the first Juliet has heard of the plan.

In secret, Juliet has married Romeo, heir of the Montague family, the implacable rivals to the Capulets. Soon thereafter Romeo was drawn into a duel with Tybalt, son of Lady Capulet's brother and Juliet's cousin. Tybalt is killed and Romeo subsequently banished upon pain of death. After one night together, the lovers parted, leaving Juliet alone. At that last separation, Juliet's "ill-divining soul" had feared that they would never meet again. She is now very close to tears, if not actually weeping.

ය80

Enter LADY CAPULET, to JULIET.

LADY CAPULET

> Ho daughter, are you up?

JULIET

> Who is't that calls? It is my lady mother.
>
> Is she not down so late or up so early?
>
> What unaccustomed cause procures her hither?

LADY CAPULET

> Why how now, Juliet?

JULIET   Madam, I am not well.   5

3 **not…late** so late getting to bed   **procures** brings
4 **unaccustomed** unusual, strange

LADY CAPULET

    Evermore weeping for your cousin's death?

    What, wilt thou wash him from his grave with tears?

    And if thou couldst, thou couldst not make him live

    Therefore have done. Some grief shows much of love

    But much of grief shows still some want of wit.   10

JULIET

    Yet let me weep for such a feeling loss.

LADY CAPULET

    So shall you feel the loss, but not the friend

    Which you weep for.

JULIET   Feeling so the loss,

    I cannot choose but ever weep the friend.

LADY CAPULET

    Well girl, thou weep'st not so much for his death   15

    As that the villain lives which slaughtered him.

JULIET

    What villain, madam?

LADY CAPULET   That same villain Romeo.

JULIET *(Aside.)*

    Villain and he be many miles asunder

    God pardon him! I do with all my heart,

    And yet no man like he doth grieve my heart.   20

LADY CAPULET

    That is because the traitor murderer lives.

JULIET

    Ay madam, from the reach of these my hands.

    Would none but I might venge my cousin's death!

10 **still** always
11 **feeling** deeply felt
12 **but not** but not be affected by
14 **friend** lover (pun)
20 **like he** as he does (by his absence)

22 **hands** (for lovemaking/for vengeance)
23 **Would . . . death!** (so Romeo would be spared/so vengeance might be fit)

LADY CAPULET

We will have vengeance for it, fear thou not.

Then weep no more: I'll send to one in Mantua   25

Where that same banished runagate doth live,

Shall give him such an unaccustomed dram

That he shall soon keep Tybalt company,

And then I hope thou wilt be satisfied.

JULIET

Indeed I never shall be satisfied   30

With Romeo till I behold him . . . Dead! . . .

Is my poor heart so for a kinsman vexed.

Madam, if you could find out but a man

To bear a poison, I would temper it

That Romeo should, upon receipt thereof,   35

Soon sleep in quiet. O how my heart abhors

To hear him named and cannot come to him

To wreak the love I bore my cousin

Upon his body that hath slaughtered him!

LADY CAPULET

Find thou the means and I'll find such a man.   40

But now I'll tell thee joyful tidings, girl.

JULIET

And joy comes well in such a needy time.

What are they, beseech your ladyship?

LADY CAPULET

Well, well, thou hast a careful father, child,

One who, to put thee from thy heaviness,   45

---

26 **runagate** fugitive
27 **unaccustomed dram** unlooked for
  dose (of poison)
29 **satisfied** (in vengeance)
30 **satisfied** repaid/sexually fulfilled
34 **temper** mix/modify

36 **sleep in quiet** die/sleep peacefully
38 **wreak** avenge/express
39 **his body that** the body of him who
44 **careful** caring
45 **heaviness** sorrow

Hath sorted out a sudden day of joy

That thou expects not nor I looked not for.

JULIET

Madam, in happy time! What day is that?

LADY CAPULET

Marry, my child, early next Thursday morn

The gallant, young, and noble gentleman,   50

The County Paris, at Saint Peter's Church

Shall happily make thee there a joyful bride.

JULIET

Now by Saint Peter's Church and Peter too,

He shall not make me there a joyful bride!

I wonder at this haste, that I must wed   55

Ere he that should be husband comes to woo.

I pray you tell my lord and father, madam,

I will not marry yet; and when I do, I swear

It shall be Romeo, whom you know I hate,

Rather than Paris. These are news indeed!   60

LADY CAPULET

Here comes your father. Tell him so yourself

And see how he will take it at your hands.

46 **sorted out** arranged   48 **in . . . time** it's the right time

CR⋈

Rehearsing the Scene

Lady Capulet comes to convey her husband's wishes; either she is a very strong and decisive woman, or one who acts only on impulse. Seeing Tybalt lying dead in the public street, she, and not her husband, had demanded that the prince should revenge his death by killing Romeo. It was she who countered Benvolio's account of what had happened with an invented and exaggerated version of her own, and called again for vengeance and Romeo's death. In this scene, Lady Capulet, who is not aware of her daughter's affection for Romeo, may be trying, rather desperately, to comfort her daughter by inventing a story about a plot to poison Romeo by "one in Mantua" (1. 25). But alternatively, she could be very controlled and purposeful, and her talk of revenge an account of a genuine and ruthless plan. Many variations are possible between these two readings. But whichever is chosen for the beginning of the scene must decide how it finishes; Lady Capulet can be glad to relinquish her task to her "careful" husband; or her praise of him at line 44 can be sarcastic, and her concluding words as he enters imply her own power over him.

Juliet is discovered in a state of inconsolable mourning, for her cousin and for Romeo's very recent departure from their marriage bed. Her words express her divided mind and feelings in many double meanings, one being appropriate to her, the other intended for her mother's ears. How conscious is Juliet of this deception, how in control of both meanings? Is she in real danger of disclosing her love for Romeo? Line 18 must be spoken aside, but her following words can be so passionate that were her mother not lost in her own thoughts, she must understand their secret meaning.

Some actresses have played Lady Capulet as a woman with the same strong passions as her daughter; having only one daughter herself and her husband being much older, she has been played as a woman with unusually strong feeling and possessiveness toward her brother's son.

After Lady Capulet changes the subject of their talk at line 41, both characters are revealed in new ways: the mother speaks with kindness, after her own fashion; Juliet with assurance and rapid, unambiguous, invention. Do either of these new "roles" come easily?

WORKING ON MODERN AND
FIRST FOLIO TEXTS

Paul Sugarman

It is important when working on text that you gain information from modern edited texts, such as the Applause Shakespeare Library, which can provide much information on understanding what is happening in the scene and then look at the original printed texts of the First Folio, such as the Applause First Folio Editions, which can give additional insights.

So on the pages that follow, we look at two of the famous speeches in the play—the Nurse's speech about raising Juliet and Mercutio's Queen Mab speech, first looking at those speeches from the Applause Shakespeare Library and then the same speeches from *Once More Unto the Speech* by Neil Freeman.

One of the most noteworthy differences is that in modern texts both of these speeches are set as verse while in the original Folio edition they were set as prose! We are often unaware of how many changes were made by editors in the effort to make Shakespeare more accessible. Another significant change is that in modern texts Juliet's parents are identified as Lord and Lady Capulet (as shown in the previous scene) while in the Folio they are referred to as Capulet and Capulet's Lady. There is no indication that the Capulets had any kind of noble title, which is why it would be so appealing to marry Juliet to the "Countie (Count) Paris" as he is a close relation to Prince Escalus.

Nurse's Speech: Modern Text

NURSE Faith, I can tell her age unto an hour.

LADY CAPULET   She's not fourteen.

NURSE   I'll lay° fourteen of my teeth—

And yet, to my teen° be it spoken, I have but four—

She's not fourteen. How long is it now   15

To Lammas-tide?°

LADY CAPULET   A fortnight and odd days.

NURSE Even or odd, of all days in the year,

Come Lammas Eve at night shall she be fourteen.

Susan° and she—God rest all Christian souls—

Were of an age. Well, Susan is with God;   20

She was too good for me. But as I said,

On Lammas Eve at night shall she be fourteen;

That shall she, marry;° I remember it well.

'Tis since the earthquake now eleven years,

And she was weaned—I never shall forget it—   25

Of all the days of the year, upon that day;

For I had then laid wormwood° to my dug,

Sitting in the sun under the dovehouse wall;

My lord and you were then at Mantua.—

Nay, I do bear a brain.° —But as I said,   30

When it did taste the wormwood on the nipple

Of my dug and felt it bitter, pretty fool,

To see it tetchy° and fall out with the dug!

"Shake,"° quoth the dovehouse! 'Twas no need, I trow,°

To bid me trudge.°   35

And since that time it is eleven years,

For then she could stand high-lone,° —nay, by th' rood,°

She could have run and waddled all about,

For even the day before she broke° her brow,

And then my husband—God be with his soul,   40

'A° was a merry man—took up the child:

"Yea," quoth he, "dost thou fall upon thy face?

Thou wilt fall backward° when thou hast more wit;°

Wilt thou not, Jule?" And, by my holidam,°

The pretty wretch left crying and said, "Ay."   45

To see now how a jest shall come about!°

I warrant, an ° I should live a thousand years,

I never should forget it. "Wilt thou not, Jule?" quoth he,

And, pretty fool, it stinted,° and said, "Ay."

wager
sorrow

August 1

(her own daughter)
the same age

by Mary

(a bitter herb)

can remember

irritable
move   I'm sure
be off

quite alone*   cross

grazed

he
i.e., for love-making
   understanding
holy thing, relic

turn out to be true
if

stopped (crying)

12–58 Lady Capulet has asked no question, but the Nurse at once assumes the role of informant. She settles to her task, probably sitting down at either line 12 or lines 15–16. The joke against herself (I.14) brings laughter (at least from herself) and establishes her, for the theater audience, as an entertainer. The question of lines 15–16 draws her onstage audience into her reveries about the past.

Although this scene until line 35 has been printed here from the imperfect first quarto, where it was printed irregularly as prose, the liveliness of the Nurse's long speech is unmistakable and allows the actress to create a dominating and varied performance. The digression about her own dead child (ll.19–21) can cast a shadow across her more robust feelings. Boasts about a good memory and her realization that she should return to her main tale with "But as I said," invite a self-conscious delivery and suggest the nurse's self-indulgence and comparative forgetfulness about her employer. Juliet is referred to as "she" or "it"; so the speech must be directed to the mother, but most actresses speak it to show that the Nurse is also counting on Juliet's avid attention.

The reported words of the Nurse's husband together with her memories of the enigmatic "shake" of the dovehouse and the calamitous earthquake, give an immediate, present-tense actuality, especially if spoken with demonstrative mimicry. The bawdy lines 43–45 provide a climax for the speech, making the Nurse helpless with laughter and provoking three repetitions, two against the express wish of Lady Capulet. Probably the Nurse should make an attempt to be silent or serious and then give in to her own instincts. At lines 53–55, she is still elaborating, as if her mind is still full of joyful and affectionate memories.

Nurse's Speech: First Folio Text

NURSE: FAITH I CAN TELL HER AGE UNTO AN HOURE .
between 1.3.11–62

Background: Juliet's age is discussed by Capulet's wife (her blood mother) and the Nurse (her milk mother). Interestingly, the Nurse lays claim to more accurate dating than Juliet's mother.

Style: as part of a three-handed scene

Where: inside or in the grounds of the Capulet residence

To Whom: Juliet's mother and Juliet

# of Lines: 38   **Probable Timing:** 1.55 minutes

Nurse

1   Faith I can tell her age unto an houre .

2   Ile lay fourteene of my teeth,
     And yet to my teene be it spoken,
     I have but foure, shee's not fourteene .

3   {*O}f all daies in the yeare come
     Lammas Eve at night shall she be fourteene .

4   Susan & she,
     God rest all Christian soules, were of an age .

5   Well Susan
     is with God, she was too good for me .

6   But as I said, on La-
     mas Eve at night shall she be fourteene, that shall she ma-
     rie, I remember it well .

7   'Tis since the Earth-quake now
     eleven yeares, and she was wean'd I never shall forget it,

of all the daies of the yeare, upon that day : for I had then
laid Worme-wood to my Dug sitting in the Sunne under
the Dovehouse wall, my Lord and you were then at
Mantua, nay I doe beare a braine .

8 But as I said, when it
did tast the Worme-wood on the nipple of my Dugge,
and felt it bitter, pretty foole, to see it teachie, and fall out
[with the] Dugge, Shake quoth the Dove-house, 'twas no
neede I trow to bid mee trudge : and since that time it is
[a eleven] yeares, for then she could stand [alone], nay bi'th'
roode she could have runne, & wadled all about : for even
the day before she broke her brow, & then my Husband
God be with his soule, a was a merrie man, tooke up the
Child, yea quoth hee, doest thou fall upon thy face ? thou
wilt fall backeward when thou hast more wit, wilt thou
not Jule ?

9 And by my holy-dam, the pretty wretch lefte
crying, & said [I] : to see now how a Jest shall come about .

10 I warrant, & I [shall] live a thousand yeares, I never should
forget it:wilt thou not [Julet] quoth he ? and pretty foole
it stinted, and said [I] .

---

11 {*} I cannot chuse but laugh, to thinke
it should leave crying, & say [I] : and yet I warrant it
had upon it brow, a bumpe as big as a young Cockrels
stone ? A perilous knock, and it cryed bitterly .

12 Yea quoth
my husband, fall'st upon thy face, thou wilt fall back
-ward when thou commest to age : wilt thou not Jule ?

13   It

stinted : and said [I] .

―――――――――――――――――――――

14 Peace I have done : God marke thee too his grace

thou wast the prettiest Babe that ere I nurst, and I might

live to see thee married once, I have my wish .

Apart from the first two sentences (possibly), Q1–4/Ff sets this speech in prose, in which she continues even beyond the key moment when Capulet's Wife as Old Lady turns the scene into verse—when she begins to discuss marriage: thus the marked contrast between the Nurse's earthy stream-of-consciousness view of life and Juliet's childlike vision both shown in the ease of prose, compared to the verse uttering of the "Old Lady's" (Juliet's mother's) more dutiful adult expectations, no matter how romantically stated, which could not be more sharply and theatrically expressed. Unfortunately, most modern texts reset the speech as verse.

• Thus, if, as the source texts suggest, the speech is in prose, then this shaded passage is probably set in irregular verse (7/9/8 syllables) and could denote something special for the Nurse: undue attention to Juliet perhaps, or gathering style and energy in preparation for the long story about to begin.

• Most modern texts not only create a more formal (verse speaking) Nurse, but they add at least fourteen extra pieces of punctuation, thus slowing the speed of her flow, especially in F #8.

• Overall, the speech is passionate (32/35), yet the start is marked by a huge swing between the opening emotion and the (quickly unsuccessful) attempt at intellectual control, while the end is marked by the sudden appearance of determined surround phrases.

• In asserting Juliet's correct age, the Nurse starts emotionally (0/6, F #1–2), but she offers the proof of "Lammas Eve" (F #3–6) somewhat more intellectually (8/4), and the further affirmation (Juliet being "wean'd" on the day of the "Earth-quake") becomes passionate (F #7, 7/7), with a lovely self congratulatory moment ending the sentence ("nay I doe beare a braine").

• The build-up to the Earth-quake ("the Worme-wood on the nipple of my Dugge") is passionate (the first four lines of F #8, 5/5), and then comes a moment of emotion at the recollection of Juliet being able to "runne" even at her early age, and the new recollection of her husband, becomes passionate once more (4/4, F #8's final four and a half lines), with the memory of the naughty joke.

> ? thou wilt fall backeward when thou hast more wit, wilt thou not
> Jule ?

is highlighted in being set as the first surround phrase of the speech, after twenty-four lines.

• And both passion and surround phrases continue as she offers various repetitions of both joke and circumstances (5/6 and six surround phrases, the ten lines of F #9–12)—a fixation on happier days when her husband was alive and Juliet a needy child dependent upon her care perhaps ...

• ... especially since this is followed by F #13, the first unembellished (and short) sentence, the calm yet determined recollection

> . It stinted: and said I .

heightened by also being set as two surround phrases.

• An unembellished monosyllabic surround phrase also marks the Nurse's final agreement to keep quiet

> . Peace I have done :

finishing with a passionate summation of Juliet's beauty as a child (2/1, F #14).

Queen Mab Speech: Modern Text

MERCUTIO O then I see Queen Mab hath been with you.
She is the fairies' midwife,° and she comes
In shape no bigger than an agate° stone   55
On the forefinger of an alderman,
Drawn with a team of little atomies°
Over men's noses as they lie asleep;
Her wagon spokes made of long spinners'° legs;
The cover,° of the wings of grasshoppers;   60
Her traces,° of the smallest spider web;
Her collars, of the moonshine's wat'ry beams;
Her whip, of cricket's bone; the lash, of film;°
Her wagoner, a small gray-coated gnat,
Not half so big as a round little worm   65
Pricked from the lazy finger of a maid.°
Her chariot is an empty hazelnut,
Made by the joiner squirrel or old grub,°
Time out o' mind the fairies' coachmakers.
And in this state° she gallops night by night   70
Through lovers' brains, and then they dream of love;
O'er courtiers' knees, that dream on curtsies° straight;
O'er lawyers' fingers, who straight dream on fees;
O'er ladies' lips, who straight on kisses dream,
Which oft the angry Mab with blisters plagues,   75
Because their breath with sweetmeats tainted are.
Sometime she gallops o'er a courtier's nose,
And then dreams he of smelling out a suit;°
And sometime comes she with a tithe pig's tail,
Tickling a parson's nose as 'a lies asleep,   80
Then he dreams of another benefice.
Sometime she driveth o'er a soldier's neck,
And then dreams he of cutting foreign throats,
Of breaches, ambuscadoes,° Spanish blades,°
Of healths five fathom deep;° and then anon   85
Drums in his ear, at which he starts and wakes,
And being thus frighted, swears a prayer or two°
And sleeps again. This is that very Mab
That plats the manes of horses in the night,
And bakes° the elflocks° in foul sluttish hairs,   90
Which once untangled much misfortune bodes.
This is the hag,° when maids lie on their backs,
That presses them and learns them first to bear,
Making them women of good carriage.°
This is she   95

i.e., she helps give birth to
men's fantasies
(on a signet ring)
tiny creatures

long-legged spiders
wagon hood
part of the harness

filament, gossamer

(maggots were said to breed in
the fingers of lazy maids)
(squirrels gnaw nuts, and
grubs bore holes in them)
royal array

bows

petition
tenth (part of the parson's
tithe or dues)

ambushes   swords
deep drinking

(to ward off evil)

cakes   tangles

evil, malicious spirit

posture/ability to bear
children

53–71 As if sensing that Romeo is indeed troubled, Mercutio forgets leaving to go to the mask. As he gives rein to his fantasies, he gains attention at once; the maskers hold back to listen, either with jeers, which are also a form of applause, or in rapt silence.

Most Mercutios speak lightly and precisely as they list the minute accoutrements of Queen Mab. There is perhaps a self-imposed contest in setting out to complete the delicate catalog. Mercutio's success may be applauded as he rounds off with lines 70–71 and ends triumphantly with "love." This in turn leads to another list, this time of the Queen's victims.

72–95 This list offers the actor the opportunity to mimic in voice and action each one of the sleepers visited by Queen Mab: so, for example, he will use a nasal, pious voice for the avaricious parson, a loud, bragging manner and alarming action for the soldier. His stage audience will respond as Mercutio grows in confidence and in pleasure at his own outrageous fantasies. He is an entertainer at ease with his audience, improvising with dazzling precision and variety. He becomes more mysterious and then, quite quickly, more bawdy (in some phrases echoing the Nurse's report of her husband's joke).

This "Queen Mab speech" is the actor's opportunity to establish the character of Mercutio. It can suggest the quickness, sensuality, and aggressive nature of his imagination, and the finesse, range, and destructive nature of his intelligence. Above all, he is seen as ringleader around whom the whole party gathers and will wait despite their eagerness to get to the ball. He is also a contestant who at once takes up Romeo's challenge. The speech can be spoken as an improvised divertissement, which Charles Kemble made "apparently as fresh to himself as to the listener"; he "abandoned himself to the brilliant and thronging illustrations which, amidst all their rapidity and fire, never lost the simple and spontaneous grace of nature in which they took rise. Mercutio's overflow of life, with its keen, restless enjoyment, was embodied with infectious spirit" (W. Marston, *Our Recent Actors* [1890], 80–81). Although this nineteenth-century actor made a wholly attractive character of Mercutio, many actors today will show bitterness, aggression, and frustration in these impulsive fantasies, as in both stage and film versions directed by Franco Zeffirelli in the 1960s.

Queen Mab Speech: First Folio Text

MERCUTIO O THEN I SEE QUEENE MAB HATH BEENE WITH YOU.
1.4.53–95

Background: Though initially agreeing to go to the Capulet feast, Romeo
is now backing out. At first teased unmercifully by his close friend Mercutio about being in love, Romeo attempts to justify himself through
a dream: being told by Mercutio "dreamers often lye," Romeo has
quickly, wittily and pointedly responded with "In bed a sleepe while
they do dreame things true," which triggers the speech.

Style: a group address

Where: in the street

To Whom: Romeo and the group, including Benvolio and "five or six
other maskers, torch-bearers"

# of Lines: 34 **Probable Timing:** 1.40 minutes

Mercutio

1   O then I see Queene Mab hath beene with you .

2   She is the Fairies Midwife, & she comes in shape no big-
     ger [then][ ] Agat-stone, on the fore-finger of an Alderman,
     drawn with a teeme of little [Atomies], [over] mens noses as
     they lie asleepe : her Waggon Spokes made of long Spin-
     ners legs : the Cover of the wings of Grashoppers, her
     Traces of the smallest [Spiders] web, her [coullers] of the
     Moonshines watry Beames, her Whip of Crickets bone,
     the Lash of Philome, her Waggoner, a small gray-coated
     Gnat, not halfe so bigge as a round little Worme, prickt
     from the Lazie-finger of a [man] .

3   Her Chariot is an emptie
     Haselnut, made by the Joyner Squirrel or old Grub, time
     out a mind, the Fairies Coach-makers : & in this state she
     gallops night by night, through Lovers braines : and then
     they dreame of Love .

4   [On] Courtiers knees, that dreame on
Cursies strait : ore Lawyers fingers, who strait : [dreamt]
on Fees, ore Ladies lips, who strait on kisses dreame,
which oft the angry Mab with blisters plagues, because their
breath with Sweet meats tainted are .

5   Sometime she gallops
ore a Courtiers nose, & then dreames he of smelling out
a sute : & somtime comes she with [ ] Tith pigs tale, tickling a Parsons nose as a lies asleepe, then he dreames of
another Benefice .

6   Sometime she driveth ore a Souldiers
necke, & then dreames he of cutting Forraine throats, of
Breaches, Ambuscados, Spanish Blades : Of Healths five
Fadome deepe, and then anon drums in his [eares], at which
he startes and wakes ; and being thus frighted, sweares a
prayer or two & sleepes againe : this is that very Mab that
plats the manes of Horses in the night : & bakes the [Elk]-
locks in foule sluttish haires, which once untangled, much
misfortune bodes,
This is the hag, when Maides lie on their backs,
That presses them, and learnes them first to beare,
Making them women of good carriage :
This is she .

Q2–4/Ff print this speech as prose; Q1 prints a much shorter version of the speech in verse. Most modern texts change the longer prose version to verse, thus spoiling the initial casualness of the major part of the speech, as well as undoing the switch in energy for the last four and a half lines of the speech, which Q2–4/Ff do print in verse (as Mercutio focuses more and more on the ugly aspect of Mab). Also, though Q2–4/Ff print the shaded section as shown, most modern texts place it after "they lie asleepe" in the fifth line of the speech, arguing that logically the description of the "Chariot" should follow on immediately after that which draws it—this does, however, make the (not necessarily warranted) assumption that Mercutio is capable of being logical at this point in the play.

• Thus, while the speech opens intellectually (33/11, F #1–3) both the extra breath thoughts and the less than logical progression of (shaded) thought suggests that his intellectualizing is far more freewheeling than most modern texts allow.

• However, as he begins to focus in on the four groups Mab blesses with her dreams ("Courtiers"—twice—and "Lawyers," never Shakespeare's favorite people, together with "Parsons," often figures of fun, and "Ladies"), so emotion starts to make more of a presence (10/6, F #4-5) as their not particularly finer qualities are listed.

• The first reference to Mab and probably himself in the throes of battle (the "Souldiers necke") is passionate (6/4, F #6's opening two lines to the first colon) but as he dreams of drink, "Healths five Fadome deepe" and then awakes "frighted" Mercutio becomes very emotional (2/8, F #6's next three lines).

• Mab and her dealings with horses and "foule sluttish haires" are passionate (2/2).

• The few surround phrases underscore the effects Mab has on most of her dreamers, first the Lovers, Courtiers, and Lawyers:

> : and then they dreame of Love . [On] Courtiers knees, that dreame on Cursies strait : ore Lawyers fingers, who strait : [dreamt] on Fees

and then with the "Souldier" and the horses,

> : Of Healths five Fadome deepe, and then anon drums in his [eares], at which he startes and wakes ; and being thus frighted, sweares a prayer or two & sleepes againe : this is that very Mab that plats the manes of Horses in the night :

• As he continues, Mercutio becomes much more intense, switching to verse to explore lovemaking and its inevitable consequence: the deflowering is described emotionally (1/3 the first two lines) while the pregnancy is handled via the only unembellished section of the speech, in which vein he would continue if Romeo does not interrupt him.